T0065684

LOVING
ROMAN CATHOLICS
Well

LARRY E MILLER

WESTBOW
PRESS®
A DIVISION OF THOMAS NELSON
& ZONDERVAN

WestBow Press books may be ordered through booksellers or by contacting:

WestBow Press
A Division of Thomas Nelson & Zondervan
1663 Liberty Drive
Bloomington, IN 47403
www.westbowpress.com
844-714-3454

ISBN: 978-1-6642-7563-8 (sc)
ISBN: 978-1-6642-7564-5 (hc)
ISBN: 978-1-6642-7562-1 (e)

Library of Congress Control Number: 2022915113

Print information available on the last page.

WestBow Press rev. date: 02/14/2024

Contents

Introduction

Among evangelicals today there are varying views about the salvation of Roman Catholic people. Many of you are hoping that your Catholic friends are indeed on their way to heaven. I can certainly understand why. Your Catholic friends and acquaintances are likely good people. They may be active in their Church; talk about Jesus; and some might be protesting at an abortion clinic. Surely, they must know Jesus Christ in a saving way. Surely, they will be in heaven with me.

Others of you may have learned more about what they believe as their way of salvation and are less confident of their salvation. I know others who are actually stunned when they discover just what the Roman Catholic Church official way of salvation really is. Since there are approximately 1.2 billion Roman Catholics worldwide, and many of you who are my readers know numbers of them, this issue needs serious consideration by every evangelical.

In 2020 I published the book *Roman Catholics: Saved or Lost?*[1] Because portions of the book were largely academic, I intently listened to the responses from serious minded "book purchasers." Some of them are former Roman Catholics and others had never been Catholics but lived within a culture with numbers of Catholic friends and neighbors.

The comments were varied, sometimes a bit humorous. One person read the book, only had one question, and expressed much appreciation because such a book is needed. Another person sort of jokingly let me know he needed a dictionary as he began reading the book. One dear lady, implying that she had begun reading the book and gave me a raised eyebrow, which I think meant some parts are difficult for her. Still others worked their way through the book, with some difficulty, and were very appreciative of it.

I became convinced that a revised and shorter version of the book would be beneficial to better serve the serious-minded evangelical Christian population. Also, we observe a decline in the evangelistic activity of many mainstream evangelicals, which ought not to be. A book on this topic needs to make its way into the hands and minds of more evangelicals making a needed contribution. Thus, this project.

I want to say this as lovingly as I can. Based on their official way of salvation, and because this is what informs most Catholic people (it is what they hear from their priests) most of them are likely not saved. I do not say this as a Pharisaical legalist or someone who hates Roman Catholic people. I love them. Some of my best neighbors are Roman Catholics.

You may be thinking, how can Larry Miller be so certain. And what gives him the right to offer such a judgment. These are fair questions. Let me tell you a bit about myself. It may sound like an inappropriate boast but I sincerely do not mean it that way. I believe I have the information, experience, and heart to speak on this topic.

Following seminary training and a few years of pastoral ministry in southwest Louisiana, in 1974 I was invited to move my family to New Orleans to engage in a church-planting venture. I responded positively. Today, some forty-five years later, I am convinced it was the right God-intended decision.

It was while ministering in that area for 30 years that I developed a deep heart concern and love for Roman Catholic people. It was while there that I explored and discovered a great deal about the official Roman Catholic Church. It was there that I discovered just what most Roman Catholic people were trusting for their eternal salvation. Honestly speaking, it was a heart-breaking experience for me. But thanks unto our great God the people in our local church were able to be a part of seeing scores and scores of Roman Catholic people come to a place of confidence in heaven as their eternal destiny.

It is my labor of love for Roman Catholic people and for you my reader friends that I have undertaken this project. It is my hope that you will experience the kind of joy expressed by the Apostle Paul to the new believers in Thessalonica. "For who is our hope or joy or crown of exultation? Is it not even you, in the presence of our Lord Jesus at His coming? For you are our glory and joy" (I Thessalonians 2:19,20).

Chapter 1

FROM HOPE TO ANGUISH

For many of you the issue of the salvation of Roman Catholic people is controversial, puzzling, and even frustrating. You have Catholic friends or family members. You know others through the normal associations of life. Even though you observe that they worship or practice their faith differently than evangelical Christians, you may believe some of them or most of them are saved and prepared for eternity. You likely hope they are. These would be normal desires. And you may even get a bit disturbed when someone else implies that this might not be so.

Comments I have heard from those within the evangelical community.

> I am engaged to a Roman Catholic person and she believes in the deity, crucifixion, and resurrection of Jesus Christ. I think she is a believer.

> I know Roman Catholics who are good persons, who take their church seriously, and believe basically what we believe. Must be a child of God.

> I participate with many Roman Catholics in pro-life marches and activities. They talk about Jesus Christ

and are in a church sponsored course on marriage. They sound like they are true Christians.

Even though our religious systems are different, how do I know what my Roman Catholic friend is trusting for salvation?

Wow! As I have learned more, I realized I did not understand what the official way of salvation was according to the Roman Catholic Church.

I did not know the Catholic Church had such control over the salvation of its participants.

What other expressions have you heard from different people?

What other thoughts have you had on the topic?

It is my experience that many evangelicals do not understand the official Roman Catholic way of salvation. Likewise, some self-proclaimed Roman Catholics do not understand it. Confusion about the salvation message is not beneficial to anyone, be he a self-proclaimed evangelical or Roman Catholic person.

The history of the Protestant and Roman Catholic churches includes deep animosities during certain time periods; animosities that are surprising to many. We may find ourselves experiencing a bit of unrest due to our lack of knowledge of church history and "salvation way" controversies. A brief overview of relevant history ought to be helpful.

FROM ANIMOSITY TO FRIENDLINESS

Catholics and non-Catholics have a history of animosity. Starting at about the fifth[th] century the Roman Catholic Church began to assert that they were the only true and authentic Christian church. Augustine (354-430) was the most highly respected saint of the Roman Catholic Church. Pope John Paul II called Augustine "the common father of our Christian civilization."[1] Augustine believed that grace was dispensed only by the Roman Catholic Church,[2] and there is no truth, no gospel, no salvation outside the one Catholic Church.[3]

Eventually most all professing Christians who were not Catholic were considered heretics, resulting in serious mistreatments and persecutions by the Roman Church. The Waldensians are one example. The group was founded around 1173 by Peter Waldo. They believed in a strict adherence to the Bible with a number of doctrines that were not common to Roman Catholic belief. These included the priesthood of all believers; the once for all atoning death of Christ providing an instantaneous justification when one believed; and a denial of transubstantiation.

In about 1180 the Catholic Church declared them heretics excommunicating them. Years of persecution followed such as burning more than eighty Waldensians at the stake in 1211 at Strasbourg. This action launched several centuries of persecution, which nearly destroyed the movement.

Additionally, even Roman Catholic Church leaders were not all in total agreement regarding all aspects of belief. Alister McGrath is highly respected for his work on the late medieval (think pre-Reformation) Roman Catholic way of salvation. There was serious confusion with a bewildering variety of answers to the crucial question, "What must I do to be saved?" Popular Pelagianism was rampant. It was widely held that salvation was something that could be earned by good works. Pelagius taught that to have salvation an individual must meet the full rigor of the demands of God and do so without God's help.

There were always leaders within the Roman Church who aimed at Reformation. Martin Luther was among them. Because he advocated salvation entirely by faith, not a salvation that required the merit of human works, he was excommunicated from the Roman Catholic Church by Pope Leo X in 1521. So yes, the Protestant Reformation happened (1517-1555).

The Council of Trent (1545-1563) was conducted by the Roman Catholic Church as a response to the Protestant Reformation. Its purpose was twofold. One, to define the doctrines of the church in reply to the *heresies of the Protestants*, [emphasis mine], and two, to bring about a thorough reform of the inner life of Roman Catholic Christians.[4] Numerous beliefs as held by the Protestants were identified as heresies which included automatic excommunication. A quick review of the Council of Trent documents yields approximately 150 "anathemas," which means wishing an eternal damnation on the heretics, the Protestants. This antagonism by the Roman Catholic Church toward Protestants continued for about four hundred years and although lessened greatly it still exists to some degree today. However, it is very important to understand that the dogmatic statements of the Council of Trent, including its 151 anathemas pronounced upon the Protestants, have not been removed from this authoritative document.

Fast forward to the early days of the United States, Roman Catholic immigrants were often seriously mistreated. There were two varieties or reasons for this mistreatment. Their version of Christianity was opposed by the mostly Protestant population with a theological heritage dating from the Protestant Reformation. The second cause was of the secular type. Could they be loyal to the United States and loyal to the Pope at the same time? An illustration of the seriousness of the derogatory opinions about Catholics was observed in Boston and New York where shops lining the streets posted signs, "No Irish need Apply," because they were considered drunkards and even barbarous. This level of derogatory attitude toward Catholics was a surprise to me and my evangelical friends when I mentioned it.

The largest number of Catholic immigrants, thirty million, occurred between 1840 and 1924. During the same time period major Protestant churches tripled in size, from five million to sixteen million members and Catholic Churches quadrupled from three million to twelve million.

Attitudes within the secular political circles began to change in the twentieth[th] century. John Kennedy was the first Catholic elected president. Today six of the nine Supreme Court Justices are Catholics.

In the religious realm the Vatican II Council (1962-1965) was a significant contributor to changing attitudes in the twentieth[th] Century. Vatican II is the title used of the Roman Catholic Church's third Ecumenical Council,[5] following Trent and Vatican I. Just what was the intent of Pope John XXII when he called the council? This question is debated to this day. However, at least two key purposes can be discerned. First, the Pope seemed to believe *renewal* was in order. The forthcoming Council will meet because of urgent need "to give greater efficiency to its sound vitality and promote sanctification of its members."[6]

Second, the *reunion* of Catholics and non-Catholics was a major purpose. "Then at the time of generous and growing efforts which are made in different parts for the purpose of rebuilding that visible unity of all Christians … ; it is very natural that the forthcoming Council should provide premises of doctrinal clarity and of mutual charity that will make still more alive in our separated brothers the wish for the hoped-for return to unity and will smooth the way."[7] Note that Roman Catholics see reunion to be a return of Protestants to the Roman Catholic Church.

Optimism regarding future Roman Catholic and Protestant relations began to surge even in some evangelical circles. John R. W. Stott penned in the foreword to David Well's book *Revolution in Rome,*

> For over four hundred years Protestants and Roman Catholics have remained in the entrenched position into which they dug themselves at the Reformation. Just about the only contact has been to lob theological grenades at one another across a deserted no man's land. The argument was largely restricted to the terms of the Reformation Confessions and the decrees of the Council of Trent. The polemics on both sides have been rigid and often harsh … Those days are over. For Rome has changed and is continuing to change.[8]

It would appear that Stott was overly optimistic. At the Vatican II Council possible changes in the Roman Catholic way of salvation were not even considered.

However overly harsh language by Catholics and Protestants alike appears to have declined and both groups seem to be pleased that non-Christian attitudes have abated to a large degree. As this trend continued more and more Protestants began to think that perhaps most Roman Catholics are saved after all but just express their faith differently. The issue of the salvation of the Roman Catholics became a debated, even controversial, issue within a broad range of self-professed Protestants. For over two hundred years since the start of evangelicalism (about 1730), the near unanimous view had been that most Roman Catholics were lost. This view is now changing among numbers of self-professed evangelicals.

Even the term evangelical is being debated today as to its meaning.[9] However, a core meaning is clear. It is from the Greek term *euaggelion* which can be pronounced like the English term "evangel." Its basic meaning is "the gospel" which speaks of the salvation of individual people. A brief definition would be salvation provided by the once for all time sufficient substitutionary death of Christ Jesus Christ for our sins and offered to us by God requiring a faith alone personal response.

WHY GREATER NUMBERS OF EVANGELICALS HAVE BEGUN TO BELIEVE THAT MOST ROMAN CATHOLICS POSSESS ETERNAL SALVATION

The factors that have contributed to these changing views about the salvation of Catholic people are several. Trans-denominationalism is defined as cooperation and participation in activities, such as evangelistic crusades, by sufficiently likeminded people of different denominational and independent church circles. Such activities required participants to overlook some lesser important distinctives of each. Perhaps as an unintended consequence to some degree this began to weaken commitment to a solid biblical gospel understanding.

Second, the needed emphasis on evangelism, including the necessity of a supernatural conversion, was a key driving force in the evangelical movement and was certainly mostly good. However, it has been observed that sometimes evangelism was so elevated that sound doctrine was reduced in importance. The result could have been lack of gospel clarity in some circles.

Third, cultural engagement was a major contributor. There is within broad evangelicalism a growing emphasis on social or cultural engagement as a necessary part of the whole gospel. In the controversial document Evangelicals and Catholics Together[10], the drafters stated in "Section IV. We (Roman Catholics and Evangelicals) Contend Together," "Christians individually and the church corporately also have a responsibility for the right ordering of civil society." [11] In this really a valid assertion? Some have quoted for support of this position this portion of 2 Corinthians 5:19, "God was in Christ reconciling the world to Himself." Any interpreter should be aware that in the New Testament the term *world* is used several different ways. It seems clear to me that the better interpretation of this verse is that individuals who are living within the earthly cosmos of humanity are reconciled by the work of God, so it is speaking of individual salvation rather than rightly ordering society.[12]

It is my view that we as evangelical Christians do have some responsibility to be engaged so as to impact the culture about us. Authors D. A. Carson[13] and Wayne Grudem[14] both so advocated and are quite helpful. So, what is the problem with cultural engagement?

On a personal level, such engagement often partners evangelicals and Roman Catholic people in the same cause, such as anti-abortion and gender issues. It is interesting to note that evangelicals and traditional Roman Catholics agree on several core issues, actually more than evangelicals and liberal Protestants might agree. While engaging we might become acquainted with individual Roman Catholics and observe them to be sincere and good people. They might talk about Jesus Christ. Some of them might be involved in a Bible study within their church. They seem to be Christians. Some of them could be. Yes, this could contribute to more evangelicals thinking that many or most Roman Catholics must be authentic believers.

Another aspect of a similar dynamic works out on a national level. In 2018, one of my favorite Supreme Court Justices, Anton Scalia, died. He was a warrior for cultural values, with which I often agreed. Following the nationally televised memorial service for Judge Scalia, some observers publicly stated with a level of celebration something like, "At the memorial service of Justice Scalia they did not bow to political correctness but chose to publicly declare the gospel." I viewed the service, and yes, they did speak about Jesus Christ and eternal life. However, at one point in the mass, conducted by the son of Judge Scalia, the sacramental elements of bread and wine were held up, sanctified by whatever process is deemed appropriate, and these words were spoken, "We now offer these for the sins of Anton Scalia."

A chill went through my body. This isn't the gospel Jesus Christ spoke of and declared by the New Testament writers, most ably defended and defined by the apostle Paul. Among other things this expressed belief denies the sufficiency of the once-for-all death of Jesus Christ to have paid the penalty for all our sins. Judge Scalia was reported to have been a devout practitioner of his religion. I don't know what he was deeply trusting for his salvation. However, such observations represent either a lack of understanding of the true biblical gospel that saves or perhaps an unwitting compromise of the gospel because of respect for this fellow culture warrior.

Yes, sometimes the growing emphasis that there has been on social action has in some circles reduced commitment to gospel clarity, even in some cases the need to spread a personal salvation message. Therefore, the arena of social action or cultural engagement, when overdone or misapplied, has contributed to the growing numbers within evangelicalism who believe that likely most Catholics are our brothers and sisters in Christ.

Fourth, just how are we to understand the term "unity" or "one" expressed five times in the prayer of Jesus Christ in John 17? One interpretation is that Jesus Christ wished for an institutional or organizational unity, meaning that all Christian communities ought to be fitted together in an earthly organization. Others understood the meaning that all such Christian communities ought to cooperate in common causes.

Edwin Blum penned what many believe to be the better, and likely the correct, understanding of this John passage. "Admittedly the divided church is in many ways a scandal. The cure, however, isn't institutional union. . . Jesus was praying for a unity of love, a unity of obedience to God and His Word, and a united commitment to His will. There are great differences between uniformity, union, and unity." [15] There is one universal church made up of all authentic believers, all of whom have been baptized "by one Spirit. . . into one body" (I Corinthians 12:13). The kind of unity spoken of by Jesus Christ is oneness defined by the truth of God. Unity that has been gained by means of a sacrifice of truth isn't worthy of the name. Can there be within broader evangelicalism a desire for some sort of unity such that the result can be a willingness to compromise gospel truth that saves?

Fifth, the current lack of interest in doctrinal clarity in general is likely the most important factor, specifically in the area of gospel clarity. Regarding truth, Jesus Christ stated, "And you will know the truth, and the truth will make you free" (John 8:32). According to Paul, the "truth" can and must be discovered. In his last written epistle, 2 Timothy, he used *truth* or similar terms at least twelve times. Note a couple of examples. "Retain the standard of sound words, which you have heard from me, in the faith and love which are in Christ Jesus. Guard, through the Holy Spirit who dwells in us, the treasure which has been entrusted to you" (2 Timothy 1:13–14). "Be diligent to present yourself approved to God as a workman who does not need to be ashamed, accurately handling the word of truth" (2 Timothy 2:15.)

Both Jesus Christ and the Apostle Paul declared truth to be a high priority issue.

Relativistic pluralism has a catastrophic impact on our culture. Briefly relativistic pluralism can be thought of as each person or group of people defining their own truth, which governs their behavior, and that none of these truths or values are inherently any more true than any others. Opposition to any form of certain or absolute truth is causing a revolution in ethics in the United States. Since the most certain view held by advocates of such a relativistic pluralism view is that there is no such thing as a certain or absolute truth, many within evangelicalism are knowingly or unknowingly impacted by this cultural landslide. It is well understood that the church often follows the culture.

In his insightful book, *The Courage to Be Protestant,*[16] David Wells asserts that a large, perhaps even the largest, factor in this indifference to doctrinal essentials was that "evangelicalism began to be infested by the culture in which it was living. And then Christianity became increasingly reduced simply to private, internal, therapeutic experience. Its doctrinal form atrophied and then crumbled."[17] In his book *Our Legacy*, John Hannah stated that "the current state of the church [he includes the evangelical church here] is that of an 'ecclesiastical swamp' . . . doctrine is the soul of the church, and the church has lost its soul."[18]

I have likely identified the major contributing factors to the precipitous change among numbers of self-proclaimed evangelicals in attitude toward the salvation of Roman Catholic people. With a decline in commitment to, and clarity of, doctrine in general, there is sure to be a parallel decline in gospel clarity. What then follows is a change and, in my view, tragic decline in opinions about the salvation of most Roman Catholic people.

For those who would like additional clarifying information about these issues my book *Roman Catholics: Saved or Lost?* pages 55-72 would be a good source.

HAVE ROMAN CATHOLIC CHANGES RESULTED IN A DIFFERENT WAY OF SALVATION FOR THEIR PEOPLE?

I do not know many Protestants or Roman Catholics who wish to return to the harsh language or abusive treatments of the past. However, the more important issue is the answer to the question, how does one gain heaven for eternity.

Though in the post-Vatican II era the Catholic Church seemed to change into a friendlier face and a more pleasant outer appearance, at its doctrinal core there have been no changes. Note the following from the 1966 Vatican II document.

> "The salient point of this Council is not, therefore, a discussion of one article or another of the fundamental doctrine of the church which has repeatedly been taught by the Fathers and by ancient and modern theologians . . . but from the renewed, serene, and tranquil adherence to all the teaching of the church in its entirety and preciseness, as it still shines forth in the Act of the Council of Trent and first Vatican Council."[19]

The Vatican II Council was intended to put a new face on the Roman Catholic Church. But if they intended to change pre-Vatican II doctrine of salvation, justification would have been discussed.

However, the word justification doesn't even appear in the index to the Vatican II documents, as translated by Abbott.

It is very important to keep this in mind. The Roman Catholic Church has not changed its views regarding the way of salvation. Their views regarding the way of salvation defined in the Council of Trent remain their official views even unto this day. In chapters two and three I present a more complete presentation of the official Roman Catholic Church way of salvation.

There continues to be some frustration among serious-minded evangelicals regarding the salvation of Roman Catholic people. I understand. I write with sensitivity toward this issue. A person is not automatically a believer because he is a member of my church, and a person is not automatically an unbeliever because he is a member of the Catholic Church. We don't always know what is happening in another person's heart. However, it seems clear to me that a gospel-denier is in need of personal salvation.

I am a conservative evangelical who has a special love for Roman Catholic people. The salvation of anyone, Protestant or Roman Catholic, depends on what the person is trusting for salvation. I want to say this as lovingly as I can, based on their official way of salvation, and because this is what informs most Catholic people (it is what they hear from their priests) most of them are likely not saved. I do not say this as a Pharisaical legalist or someone who hates Roman Catholic people. I love them. Some of my best neighbors have been Roman Catholics.

The "group" that invited me to New Orleans to join them in a church planting effort had been meeting for several months in a Bible study environment but also praying and discussing the need for this new church in New Orleans. The group was small (eleven charter members when officially organized) but highly committed.

One of the values of the group was that the church would be healthy and balanced. There was a strong commitment to biblical truth (doctrine) and a pulpit characterized by solid Bible exposition. The name Berean (from Acts 17:11) was an adjective in the church name. I also noted they had observed that even though some churches may include this emphasis, they often lacked intentional and effective evangelism, so the latter was to be an intentional goal of our group. And this church was going to be planted in New Orleans with an approximate ninety percent Roman Catholic population. This balanced perspective appealed to me.

Through the enablement of our great God, we were able to develop and pursue evangelistic methodology, which resulted in scores and scores of Roman Catholic people discovering that salvation is a gift and not a reward. Eventually two-thirds of the people in our church were from a Roman Catholic background. To this day I weep when I replay some of the testimonies of these serious-minded people.

In 1993 I did a research project toward a Doctor of Ministry degree which included surveying four hundred former Roman Catholics involved in evangelical churches in South Louisiana. The major goal was to determine from the perspective of these former Roman Catholics what methods were most effective and helpful toward them understanding the biblical grace gospel that saves. I don't know of another project like this that has been done. Also, I have conducted numerous seminars in local churches and with regional pastor groups. I have also done such training in Eastern Europe, where the dominant religion is Eastern Orthodox.

In my early years as a pastor in New Orleans I read the 1975 *The Catholic Catechism* book authored by John Hardon,[20] wanting to find out how I might have eternal life if I was a practicing Catholic. To this day I remember when I came to a certain place in the book. Please read the following carefully.

The Church's magisterium would understandably not be silent in a matter of such great significance (eternal punishment). In what has come to be known as the Athanasian Creed, . . the opening article introduces the most important truths of revelation and read, "Whoever wishes to be saved must, above all, keep the Catholic faith; for unless a person keeps this faith whole and entire he will undoubtedly be lost forever." The closing article referring to Christ's second advent affirms, "At his coming, all men are to arise with their own bodies; and they are to give an account of their lives. Those who have done good will go into eternal life; and those who have done evil will go into everlasting first."[21]

How would one know whether he or she has kept "the faith whole and entire?" Just what evil is bad enough to cause one to "go into everlasting fire?" This issue becomes more complicated when the concept of purgatory is included.

And what is the nature and purpose of purgatory? Before the end of times, Catholicism believes there is still prospect for the expiation [My addition: extinguishing guilt] opportunity called "purgatory," because its function is to purify those who die in God's friendship but are not fully cleansed of the effects of their sins."[22]

In more concrete terms, in what has been carved out of centuries of the church's reflection on revelation, there exists purgatory, in which the souls of the just who die with the stains of sin are cleansed by expiation before they are admitted to heaven. They can also be helped by the intercession of the faithful on earth.[23]

How does one die "cleansed" or without the "stain of sin"? The answers given by Hardon are shocking. "When we speak of 'stains of sin,' the expression is consciously ambivalent."[24] He further expounds regarding this subject. "It first means … it may also mean … The Church has never pronounced on this second matter."[25]

I wept when I read these pages in Hardon's *Catechism*. This is unbelievable. Cleansing or the absence of the "stain of sin" at death is what determines whether one goes to purgatory and then to heaven. However, an adequate description of this stain of sin isn't included; it is left *"consciously ambivalent"* [emphasis mine]."[26]

So, it seems that a Roman Catholic person, believing the official dogma of the church, couldn't be certain of his or her destiny. How long must one stay in purgatory? Silence. This explains why Roman Catholic funerals induce such sadness.

I hope you can understand why I feel so passionate about the needs of these dear people and why I am confident regarding my understanding of their faulty way of salvation.

Also, here let me say that confusion about the way of salvation, thus a hindrance to certain "peoples" about eternal life, is not limited to Roman Catholics. In addition to the 1.2 billion Roman Catholics there are approximately 300-500 million Eastern Orthodox people with a way of salvation very similar to that of Roman Catholicism. In addition, there are approximately 800 million self-proclaimed Protestants. Respected researcher George Barna has indicated that a significant per cent of people who identify as Protestants do not believe the clear biblical way of salvation.[27]

There are approximately 1.4 billion Muslims on planet earth. But there are likely more pseudo-Christians that need to be evangelized than there are Muslims. I have found these numbers to be surprising to many people.

A BEGINNING INQUIRY REGARDING WHAT CATHOLICS BELIEVE AS THEIR WAY TO HEAVEN

You may say but my Roman Catholic friends may not believe in the official Roman Catholic way of salvation. You are likely correct that some of them may have gotten beyond the deficient way of salvation championed by the Catholic Church and are actually by faith alone trusting Jesus Christ as Savior. Now regarding you and your friends, I suggest that you lovingly explore what or who they are actually trusting for their salvation. Here is a list of questions you could ask to see what answer they might give.

- Are you certain you would go to heaven when you die? Would you like to be certain?
- If you ae trying to be good enough to get to heaven, how will you know when you have been good enough? Or done enough good works?
- Do you believe you have sufficiently solved your sin problem(s)?
- How would you explain the way to get to heaven?
- How do you understand that you could avoid purgatory?
- What would happen to you if you stopped participating in the Eucharist?
- If God would ask you, "why should I allow you into Heaven," how would you respond?
- If you feel that it is appropriate at some point, ask what would you say if the Roman Catholic Church believed and taught something contrary to scripture?

What else could you think of?

We have learned that it is important to understand how certain terms are understood differently by evangelicals and Roman Catholics. When I conducted seminars and training session on this topic, I asked the participants for feedback. The information below regarding different term understandings was almost always considered among the most helpful.

On one occasion I was training the Campus Crusade ministry staff at the LSU campus in Baton Rouge, LA. When I began to discuss these terms, one of the young staffers almost shouted out, "That explains it." She explained that she had been asking students, numbers of whom were Roman Catholics, whether they had received Christ, and many said yes. Yet they had no interest in Bible study or discipleship. She now realizes that when they said they had received Christ, they meant that every Sunday during mass they received Christ.

DIFFERENT MEANING OF TERMS

Term	RCC Teaching	Evangelical Understanding
Born again	Water baptism	Impartation of new life
Receive Christ	At weekly communion (mass)	When one first trusted Christ as Savior
Saved by grace	Merited favor	Unmerited favor
Faith	Believing in God and what the RCC says	Believing and relying on the Bible
Good works	Activities meriting salvation	Activities in appreciation for salvation
Why did Christ die?	Establish RCC sacraments	Substitutionary and sufficient atonement
Deity of Christ	Son of Mary, Mother of God	Son of God
Forgiveness of sins	After all penance paid and purgatory experienced	At moment of saving trust
Justification	Gradual infusion of righteousness	Point-in-time declaration of Righteousness

A PAUSE

Let's hit pause for a moment. Just recently one of my good friends at our church asked me, "Have you gotten any push back?" referring to my book *Roman Catholics: Saved or Lost?* My friend did not divulge what she was thinking. But perhaps she was dealing with the anguish of thinking that so many Catholics might not be Christians after all. I completely understand that. What person in his right mind would wish that 1.2 billion Roman Catholics would spend eternity in eternal condemnation? This is certainly not my wish.

Essentially every version of "Christians" has believed that there is an eternal life and that there are different kinds of life options before us—one that is desirable and better, often called heaven; and the other not desirable and much worse, often called hell. For serious minded people the issue before us is just how we escape hell and experience heaven—for eternity?

For those of us who accept the holy scriptures, the Bible, as an accurate and authoritative revelation from God, this is the source to which we go for an answer to this most important question. We find that the Apostle Paul has given the most compete answer to our question in Romans and a more concise definition and description in Galatians. And this message is quite clear. I summarize it in chapter four.

Our next question then becomes does the official Roman Catholic way of salvation agree or disagree with the Apostle Paul way. I summarize the official Roman Catholic way of salvation in the next two chapters. Honesty requires me to conclude that it is **different** from that penned by Paul. There is nothing within me that desires such a conclusion except to accept the holy scriptures as final authority and to understand them as accurately as possible.

We then are left with two questions. Is there more than one way of salvation? Secondly, just what is an individual Roman Catholic person trusting for salvation? One could ask Protestants the same question. In other words, assuming I have understood the official Roman Catholic way of salvation, could there be individual practicing Roman Catholics who are actually trusting the saving gospel as penned by Paul? The answer would seem to be yes that is possible. I have known a few who I believe can be so described. However, throughout 45 years of ministry in predominate Roman Catholic culture in South Louisiana, and an extensive effort to understand what they believe, I am forced to conclude that the vast majority of Roman Catholic people are most impacted by the way of salvation as believed by the official Roman Catholic Church and repeatedly proclaimed by their local priests. Therefore, they are "lost" and need salvation, which is real and eternal.

So what does their church teach them about the way of salvation?

Chapter 2

ANOTHER GOSPEL: AUTHORITY AND SACRAMENTALISM

AUTHORITY AND SACRAMENTALISM

We each need to understand the official Roman Catholic way of salvation. This is something most often not understood by evangelical Christians and often not fully understood by Catholic people. Based on my experience it is that which most impacts the typical Roman Catholic person's understanding of the way of salvation. It is what they hear from their priests on a regular basis. It may be surprising, even shocking, to some of you.

Investigating what Roman Catholics believe can sometimes be a perplexing pursuit. Statements by moderate Jesuit theologian Avery Dulles illustrate what seems to be double-talk. "We [Protestants and Roman Catholics] do not greatly disagree on the way in which the individual comes to justification through grace accepted in faith. That's pretty much common doctrine between churches, even though it has not been recognized as common doctrine. Many Catholics are astonished to hear this—they think that Catholics are justified by their good works. But that has never been Catholic teaching."[1]

On the other hand, he declares, "It could be said that faith itself is intrinsically characterized by love. As I mentioned, Vatican II speaks of faith as a loving obedience, and in that sense you could say faith alone is sufficient to justify."[2]

Later in the same interview, he says, "Yes, we can merit salvation provided that we persevere in grace."[3]

However, what is declared in their official documents is clear and easy enough to understand. Utilizing their primary authoritative documents, The Council of Trent, Vatican II, and the 1995 *The Catechism of the Catholic Church,*[4] I will present the major issues that clarify their way of salvation. The central issues to understand are authority, sacramentalism, justification, and grace and faith.

What these documents declare is not that difficult to understand. You need to think your way through the following brief summary of the Roman Catholic official views on this subject. Please, I beseech you to do so. It is very important indeed.

AUTHORITY

The difference in the way of salvation for Roman Catholics begins with a different view of authority. We evangelicals understand the holy scriptures to be our final authority and we see the scriptures as a static and non-expandable revelation from God. There is no additional revelation from God and there is no other authority for way of salvation truth.

The Roman Catholic Church has a very different understanding of authority. A review of their authority system informs us of three primary pillars-apostolic succession, tradition, and biblical interpretation.

APOSTOLIC SUCCESSION

The official Roman Catholic dogma emphatically declares that the *apostolic authority* to govern the church belongs to the pope and bishops. "This sacred synod [Vatican II] teaches that by divine institution bishops have succeeded to the place of the apostles as shepherds of the Church, and that he who hears them, hears Christ ... For in virtue of his office, that is, as Vicar of Christ and pastor of the whole Church, the Roman Pontiff has full, supreme, and universal power over the Church. And he can exercise this power freely."[5]

This is consistent with the earlier Council of Trent and continues so even unto this day. Note this 1995 Catechism statement.

> The Church is apostolic. She is built on a lasting foundation, "the twelve apostles of the Lamb" (Rev. 21:14). She is indestructible (cf. Mt 16:18). She is upheld infallibly in the truth: Christ governs her through Peter and the other apostles, who are present in their successors, the Pope and the college of bishops ... The sole Church of Christ in the Creed we profess to be the one, holy, catholic, and apostolic ... *subsists in the Catholic Church* [emphasis mine; they mean Roman Catholic Church], which is governed by the successor of Peter and by the bishops in communion with him.[6]

If one looks for the "real power" of the Roman Catholic Church, it may be found in the concept of apostolic succession.[7] It gives the pope and bishops ultimate and almost total authority within the church in all doctrine and practice. And yes, the documents mean what they appear to say.

TRADITION

Tradition is considered the second pillar of their authority structure.

The Roman Catholic Church declares that it respects sacred scripture. "God is the author of Sacred Scripture. The divinely revealed realities, which are contained and presented in the text of Sacred Scripture, have been written down under the inspiration of the Holy Spirit."[8] However, a major difference is their understanding that the Bible is a beginning point for truth.[9] The conservative Protestant view has consistently believed that the scriptures provide a static, non-expandable foundation, from which the validity of the development of doctrine can be determined.

The Roman Catholic view is that the Bible is the beginning point for truth and authoritative truth is found in their own traditional practices and beliefs *even when these beliefs and practices disagree with holy scripture.*

Note carefully:

> Sacred Scripture is the speech of God as it is put down in writing under the breath of the Holy Spirit. And [Holy] (sic) *Tradition* transmits *in its entirety* [emphasis mine] the Word of God which has been entrusted to the apostles by Christ the Lord and the Holy Spirit. It transmits it to the successors of the apostles so that, enlightened by the Spirit of truth, they may faithfully preserve, expound, and spread it abroad by their preaching.[10]

> Consequently, it is not from Scripture alone that the Church draws her certainty about everything which has been revealed. Therefore, both sacred

tradition and sacred scripture are to be accepted and venerated with the same sense of devotion and reverence … Sacred tradition and sacred scripture form one sacred deposit of the Word of God, which is committed to the Church.[11]

In addition to these statements, and others that could be included, other elements added to their concept of tradition as authoritative. One such element is referred to as the faithful's "supernatural sense of the faith."[12] It is thought that the faithful "cannot error in matters of belief."[13] This means that what had come to be believed by many of the faithful is to be considered a trustworthy witness to the authentic Catholic faith. This illustrates their expansionist view of scripture.

During the Middle Ages, approximately 600-1500, tradition came into full swing when the Rome canon lawyers and theologians admitted that all the truths actually held by the church couldn't be found explicitly or implicitly in holy scripture. "To rectify this considerable deficit in terms of both earlier church history and generous scriptural support for some theological issues, a deficit that was at times even embarrassing to some of them, medieval theologians such as Rabanus Maurus simply appealed to the tradition itself, or by implication, to the Holy Spirit as the guarantee of the tradition, thereby lacing a sacred canopy—to borrow a phrase from Peter Berger—over some of what, in effect, was simply all-too-human teaching. How do we know that such is merely human teaching? It is at variance with the clear teaching of sacred scripture."[14]

And these additional "tradition based" viewpoints contribute toward the development of a way of salvation which is contrary to holy scripture. I provide an expanded presentation of this issue in my book *Roman Catholics: Saved or Lost?*[15]

A REVEALING ILLUSTRATION

In this project I am choosing to focus on the issues of authority, sacramentalism, justification and grace and faith without "detouring" into other issues such as the RCC views on Mary. However, my thinking was interrupted when on March 26, 2022, in the local newspaper, I noted the headline article "Praying for Peace." The local bishop, along with the Pope and Roman Catholics worldwide were assembling for a special prayer for Ukraine and Russia. My first thought was positive, yes this topic and the millions of people impacted needs such prayerful attention. BUT THEN I read about the local bishop praying "an Act of Consecration, entrusting Russia and Ukraine to the Immaculate Heart of Mary." My emotions were immediately transformed from encouragement to disbelief. Why would anyone entrust the Ukrainian and Russian people to anyone other than God. Also, I began to do a bit of review regarding what they mean by the "Immaculate Heart of Mary."[16]

The Immaculate Conception refers to Mary's conception, not to Christ's conception or to the virgin birth of Christ. According to the 1995 Roman Catholic *Catechism,* "Mary . . . was preserved from all stain of original sin and by a special grace of God committed no sin of any kind during her whole life."[17]

Since the mid-nineteen[th] century there has been a growing worldwide movement toward increased devotion to Mary. Pope John Paul II's devotion to Mary has become typical of recent Popes. One of the most significant "Mary" documents was penned by Pope Pus IX (1846-1878). In his 1854 declaration, *Ineffabilis Deus* (meaning the great God) he defines Mary's Immaculate Conception. He did so speaking *ex cathedra* which means it is to be considered infallible truth for the Roman Catholic Church to this day.

We declare, pronounce, and define that the doctrine which holds that the most Blessed Virgin Mary, in the first instant of her conception, by a singular grace and privilege granted by the Almighty God, in view of the merits of Jesus Christ, the Savior of the human race, was preserved free from all stain of original sin, is a doctrine revealed by God and therefore to be believed firmly and constantly by all the faithful.[18]

All of the above is without any scriptural support. I do need to add here that on some occasions Protestants have not given Mary her proper due. Note in Luke 1:28, the angel said to her, "Greetings, favored one! The Lord is with you." Yes, she, and she alone, was chosen by God to be the biological mother of Jesus. Think about Mary, and Joseph also, as they walked the dusty streets of Nazareth. Mary began to display the evidence of her pregnancy. Can't you see and hear what the townspeople must have thought and whispered. But Mary was willing to face such because she "believed God." From my viewpoint Mary should be one of the respected women of scripture. She is pictured as a faithful, humble servant of God (Luke 1:38, 46-55).

However, she was not as declared to be the Roman Church. She was not a sinless saint. Romans 5:12 declares that all mankind have sinned, with no exceptions. The Bible teaches that the only One who has ever lived on the earth without sin was the Lord Jesus Christ (II Corinthians 5:21; I Peter 2:22; I John 3:5). In Romans chapter three Paul wrote, "all have sinned and fall short of the glory of God"(23); "There is none righteous, not even one"; "There is none who does good, there is not even one" (vss. 10,12).

Additionally, Mary acknowledged she was a sinner needing salvation. "My soul exalts the Lord, and my spirit has rejoiced in God my Savior" (Luke 1:46,47).

One may hear the Catholic priest repeat the words about Mary, "Hail, full of grace, the Lord is with thee: blessed art thou among women." They will say the phrase "full of grace" supports the view that Mary was never subject to the curse. However, according to respected scholars the phrase 'full of grace" is not in the original text of scripture.[19] You will likely not find it in any translations that you read.

Enough! Thus we note one major way the Roman Catholic Church hierarchy has distorted, even contradicted, the truths of holy scripture. They do so through their confidence in "Tradition" as their ultimate authority.

HERMENEUTICS OR BIBLE INTERPRETATION

The Roman Catholic Church approach to *Bible interpretation* is considered the third pillar of their authority structure. Whatever the Roman Catholic Church says a passage of scripture means is considered to be an infallible interpretation. "The task of authentically interpreting the word of God, whether written or handed on, has been entrusted exclusively to the living teaching office of the Church."[20] "According to the saying of the Fathers, Sacred Scripture is written principally in the Church's heart rather than in documents and records, for the Church carries in her Tradition the living memorial of God's Word, and it is the Holy Spirit who gives her the spiritual interpretation of the Scripture."[21]

This teaching authority of the church resides in the *Magisterium* from the Latin word for *master*. This *Magisterium* is made up of the bishops of the church who they believe have been appointed by God Himself to be the teachers of the Catholic faith. Furthermore, it is believed that when they interpret and teach regarding faith or morals they do so with infallibility, that is without error. And Catholics are to obey the bishops even as they would Christ Himself. [22]

As an example to demonstrate the fallacy of such an authoritative position consider that the Roman Church eventually declared Mary to be the "ever-virgin" or sometimes referred to as her perpetual virginity, meaning she remained a virgin for her entire life.

> The deepening of faith in the virginal motherhood led the church to confess Mary's real and perpetual virginity even in the act of giving birth to the son of God made man. In fact, Christ's birth did not diminish his mother's virginal integrity but sanctified it. And so the liturgy of the church celebrates Mary as *Aeiparthenos,* the Ever-virgin.[23]

A quick review of several scripture passages when normally understood indicate otherwise. Note Matthew 1:24,25, "Joseph kept her a virgin . . . until she gave birth to a son." Also, when Jesus showed up in his hometown and began teaching the responses included "Is not this the carpenter's son? Is not His mother called Mary, and His brothers, James and Joseph and Simon and Judas? And His sisters, are they not all with us?" (Mark 6:3).

These three—apostolic succession, tradition, and hermeneutics—are the pillars supporting the Roman Catholic doctrinal system. For the Roman Catholic Church doctrinal truth can be found in and be determined by sources beyond the Bible.

Implications based on their view of authority.

- The Roman Catholic viewpoint is that Peter became the first Pope and when the Pope speaks *ex cathedra* ("from his chair") and when doing so with the intent to demand irrevocable assent from the entire church, he is infallible. However biblical evidence for Peter becoming the first Pope is lacking. To the contrary note Luke 22:24-30; II Corinthians 12:11; Galatians 2:11-14; Acts 15:1-35; Acts chapters 13-28 where Paul is prominent. And the early church history does not support this assumption.

- If I am convinced there is an eternal existence the major question is where to find the answer to the way to experience the best option, which is heaven itself. It is clear that for Roman Catholics the source of truth is their own tradition rather than scripture. Example: A friend of mine graduated from Jesuit High School in New Orleans, perhaps the most exclusive private high school in the city. He related to me this account of his senior year experience. A Roman Catholic priest visited each class and warned them against reading the Bible because it would confuse them. He further stated, "We will tell you what to believe."

- Whatever the Pope and the college of bishops say is required for salvation must be accepted and believed by the Roman Catholic person. Their view is that their Magisterium, or teaching authority of the church, interprets scripture infallibly, or without error. Therefore, whatever the official Roman Catholic Church says is the way of salvation is to be accepted by all the Roman Catholic lay people. In many ways today Catholics can be called cafeteria Catholics, which is Catholic in the way they prefer. However, when it comes to their salvation it has been my experience that the official position of the RC Church regarding the way of salvation is the single greatest influence on what the Roman Catholic people believe.

SACRAMENTALISM

For the Roman Catholic Church sacramentalism is at the core of their way of salvation and church systems and practices. According to the *Catechism,* Jesus Christ established seven sacraments. "The whole liturgical life of the Church revolves around the Eucharistic sacrifice and the sacraments. There are seven sacraments in the Church: Baptism, Confirmation or Chrismation, Eucharist, Penance, Anointing of the Sick, Holy Orders, and Matrimony."[24] "Adhering to the teaching of the Holy Scriptures, to the apostolic traditions, and to the consensus of the Fathers, we profess that the sacraments of the new law were all instituted by Jesus Christ our Lord."[25]

Further, "The Church affirms that for believers the sacraments of the new Covenant are necessary for salvation."[26] Note their view of the *sacrament of baptism.* Baptism by water into the Catholic Church, normally by a bishop or a priest,[27] makes one a Christian.[28] It removes original sin[29] and starts one on the way toward heaven. So, one can become a Christian only through water baptism by an ordained Catholic priest or, of necessity, by someone else.

Furthermore, they believe each sacrament is the instrumental cause of grace believed to flow from God through the Roman Catholic Church into the life of the sacrament participant. "By the action of Christ and the power of the Holy Spirit they make present efficaciously the grace that they signify."[30] They mean that their approved leaders have the authority to bring into the lives of the recipients the blessings and graces intended. They are "efficacious" because in them Christ himself is at work; it is he who baptizes, he who acts in his sacraments in order to communicate the grace that each sacrament signifies. This is the meaning of the church's affirmation that the sacraments act *ex opere operato* (literally: by the very fact of the actions being performed). This means that because of the priest's ordained position when he offers the sacraments speaking the right words, the recipient receives the grace benefits intended by the sacrament. This does not depend on the character of the priest or the faith of the recipient.

Lest you think I am exaggerating or not understanding the official Roman Catholic view, note this February 16, 2022, Associated Press headline, "Baptisms by Arizona priest presumed invalid due to error." A priest who had served in Arizona for 16 years had baptized thousands repeating incorrect wording for baptisms. The priest's error was in saying "We baptize you in the name of the Father, and of the Son, and of the Holy Spirit," when he should have begun the sentence by saying, "I baptize you." The difference is perceived to be theologically crucial because it is not the "we" of the congregation doing the baptizing but the "I" of Jesus Christ, working through the priest. In June 2020 the Vatican issued an official position stating that the "We" formula was invalid and that anyone who was baptized using it must be rebaptized.

They are saying the sacraments such as baptism must be done with precisely the right words. And baptism is perceived to remove original sin which is required to start a person on a journey toward heaven. Without a valid baptism their eternal destiny remains in jeopardy. So, thousands are being rebaptized, or one could say attempting to experience the initial proper baptism. Yes, the Roman Catholic Church is serious about these views.

Now moving on to the Eucharist which is considered the central Christian sacrament. " …the Eucharist occupies a unique place as the Sacrament of sacraments: all the other sacraments are ordered to it as to their end."[31] The term Eucharist itself is based on the Greek term *eucharisteo,* translated "thanks" in I Corinthians 11:24. However, this ends any commendation I can give to the Roman Catholic Church for its sacrament of The Eucharist. For any Roman Catholics reading this material this will sound like strange words indeed, even perhaps profane to you. But I beg all readers to follow my heart and words.

We conservative bible-based evangelicals consider the Cross event of Jesus Christ with the greatest awe, respect and worship. A central plank in our doctrine of salvation is the truth that Jesus Christ died a once for all death to pay for the sins of mankind for all time thereby satisfying the just demands of God.

In the Book of Hebrews (5:1-10:39) our Lord Jesus Christ is presented and described as superior to the Old Testament priesthood including offering a better sacrifice (9:15-10:18) than those so often repeated Old Testament sacrifices. For centuries the blood of goats and rams ran thick in the temple court. For centuries, the high priest offered blood on the horns of the golden altar to atone for the sins of the many. Sacrifice upon sacrifice. Until at last, Christ offered for all times a single sacrifice for sins.

The Greek term *hapax*, which means "once," is used five times in Hebrews chapters nine and ten. When it is used to refer to the uniqueness of Christ's Cross work it means something that cannot be repeated.[32]

In Hebrew 9:27–28, the author declares, "And inasmuch as it is appointed for men to die once and after this comes judgment, so Christ also, having been offered once [*hapax*] to bear the sins of many, will appear a second time for salvation without reference to sin, to those who eagerly await Him." This "second time" will be

His future Second Coming back to planet earth and that coming will not be to pay for sin.

As certain as it is that men die once, it is likewise certain that Christ was to be offered only once as a sacrifice for sin, for our sin(s).

The Hebrews 10:10–12 verses provide additional powerful insight. "By this will we have been sanctified through the offering of the body of Jesus Christ once for all. And every priest stands daily ministering and offering time after time the same sacrifices, which can never take away sins; but He, having offered one sacrifice for sins for all time, SAT DOWN AT THE RIGHT HAND OF GOD."

Substitutionary sacrifices offered by the Old Testament priesthood were only temporary; thus, day after day and year after year, they continued the practice, never permanently solving the sin problem. But Jesus Christ as priest and sacrifice did it once and then "sat down," because the necessary sacrificial work was accomplished—totally and finally.[33]

Several respected commentators understand these passages in this manner. Regarding Hebrews 9:24–26, Hodges states, "The heavenly ministry of Christ called for a thoroughly sufficient, one-time sacrifice. This is precisely why He appeared once for all [hapax]."[34] Regarding Hebrews 9:27–28, Hodges further states,

> With this observation (of vss. 24–25), eschatological realities come into focus. Humans are sinful creatures destined to die once, and after that to face judgment. But this danger is turned aside by the fact that Christ was sacrificed once (*hapax,* cf. v. 26) to take away the sins of many people. The recurrence of "once" (9:26, 28) and of "once for all" (7:27; 9:12; 10:10) stresses the finality and the

singleness of Christ's sacrificial work in contrast with the repeated Levite ministrations. In addition, the "once"—sacrifice of Christ (vv. 26, 28) compares with the "once"—death of each person (vs 27).[35]

This would be the common conservative evangelical view of these portions in Hebrews. And this is clearly what the biblical text is saying.

Additionally, a remembrance of these famous words by Jesus Christ on the Cross adds additional support to the idea that Jesus Christ died once and once for all time to pay the penalty for sin. He proclaimed, "*It is finished!*" (John 19:30). This is the translation of the one Greek word *tetelestai*. Papyri receipts for taxes have been recovered with this single word written across them meaning "paid in full." Jesus Christ had paid the full price for our redemption.

The "once for all" death of Christ was sufficient to pay for the sins of mankind for all time. Efforts at rejecting the sufficiency of His one death and even attempting to add meritorious works to earn salvation have been described by unmistakably disapproving terms. Note in Hebrews 10:29 an effort to do so is behaving like one who has "trampled under the foot the Son of God." This phrase "trampled under foot" "denotes contempt of the most flagrant kind."[36]

It is incredible to me that anyone within Christendom would affirm that the once for all death of Christ is not sufficient to have paid the penalty for all of our sins.

It is incredible to me that anyone within Christendom would seek to add to this one death of Christ any kind of religious practice, any work(s), anything in order to merit eternal life.

God the Father is saying, "I have offered my Son!" How can anyone say, "It is not enough."

And yet we find these descriptions and definitions of the Eucharist as understood and practiced by the Roman Catholic Church. They clearly do not believe that the once for all sacrifice of Christ was enough to have appeased the wrath of God through a satisfactory one-time payment. Here I present just a few examples. For a more complete treatment of the subject consult the book *The Gospel According to Rome* by James C. McCarthy.[37]

The Catholic Church believes that the bread and wine of communion, when properly consecrated, are transubstantiated, or the substances are actually changed into the body and blood of Jesus Christ.

> By the consecration the transubstantiation of the bread and wine into the Body and Blood of Christ is brought about. Under the consecrated species of bread and wine Christ himself, living and glorious, is present in a true, real, and substantial manner: His Body and His Blood, with his soul and his divinity.[38]

Appeasement of God is considered a central effect of the Eucharist, or the Sacrifice of the Mass. The wrath of God is being soothed.

Referring to the Eucharist—

> . . . that the Church might have a perpetual Sacrifice, by which our sins might be expiated, and our heavenly Father, oftentimes grievously offended by our crimes, might be turned away from wrath to mercy, from severity of just chastisement to clemency.[39]

Expiated means atone for guilt or sin.

And the Roman Catholic participant must repeatedly and continually offer this sacrifice. Ron Rhodes includes an insightful word about comments made by Pope John Paul II. [40]

> The Church is the instrument of man's salvation. It both contains and continually draws upon the mystery of Christ's redemptive sacrifice. Through the shedding of His own blood Jesus Christ constantly "enters into God's sanctuary thus obtaining eternal redemption" (Hebrews 9:12).

Ron Rhodes includes these keen observations regarding this quote from the pope's book.

- The biblical text of Hebrews 9:12 reads, "Through His own blood, He entered the holy place once for all, having obtained eternal redemption." "Entered" is an aorist (past) tense in the Greek, indicating a one-time past event. Yet the pope renders it in the present tense, "enters."

- Though the wording of Hebrews 9:12 is changed from what is recorded in scripture, the pope puts it in quotation marks, implying that the source of His words is in fact Hebrews 9:12.

- The pope adds "constantly" ("constantly 'enters into God's sanctuary'") and leaves out "once for all."

- The pope changes the once-for-all "*having obtained* eternal redemption" so that it reads, "*thus obtaining* eternal redemption (emphasis added).

All this changes the meaning of the biblical text. The way the pope renders the verse, it comes out sounding as though it supports the Mass. But in reality the pope has changed what the Scripture says.

This is a huge issue and ought not be ignored by a person who is serious minded about way of salvation issues.

Their view of *Christ and the church as one* greatly clouds and confuses the gospel message at the lay level.[41] It appears that for the Catholic Church *ecclesiology* (church) *replaces biblical soteriology* (way of salvation), meaning for them the way of salvation is through, and only through, these practices of the church through its bishops and priests. It also appears that the Roman Catholic Church replaces Christ as the mediator between God and man.

The individual Roman Catholic person must keep returning to the Roman Catholic system and the sacraments for any hope of eternal life. As the sacraments are experienced, grace and righteousness are understood to flow into the soul of the recipient. This is independent of his or her level of faith.

"The medieval church (600-1500) wielded massive power because, according to its own statements, it controlled the means of grace."[42]

Some implications restated.

- The Roman Catholic Church, and the church alone, has the means to bring salvation to individual people.

- This salvation requires the people to continue to return to the church and receive the benefits intended via the sacraments.

- The Eucharist is the apex of Catholic sacraments. The Catholic Church teaches that all practicing Catholics need to regularly and continually participate in the supposed ongoing resacrifice of Christ as a hoped for way to appease

God and receive forgiveness of their sins so they can enter heaven, perhaps or probably by way of purgatory.

To you my reader friends you may feel yourself challenged to consider that the above might be what your Catholic friends are believing. Perhaps there are some that might believe otherwise. I would wish that to be true. However, it has been my experience that most of them believe what the official Roman Catholic Church views are as expressed by their priests.

My response is deep sadness for so many serious-minded Catholic people.

So yes, the serious-minded evangelical who desires to lovingly and intentionally reach out to the Roman Catholic person with the biblical way of salvation is faced with a daunting task. However, keep in mind the powerful ministry of God the Holy Spirit, including the enlightenment He brings through the Word of God, the Bible.

Chapter 3

ANOTHER GOSPEL: JUSTIFICATION, GRACE AND FAITH

JUSTIFICATION

As evangelicals we believe the right understanding of justification by faith is central to the "authentically Christian" question.

Alister McGrath stated that "the Protestant doctrines of justification were established by the year 1540." He summarized the doctrines as follows:

1. Justification is the forensic *declaration* that the Christian is righteous, rather than the process by which he or she is *made* righteous. It involves a change in *status* rather than in *nature*.

2. A deliberate and systematic distinction is made between justification (the external act by which God declares the believer to be righteous) and sanctification or regeneration (the internal process of renewal by the Holy Spirit.)

3. Justifying righteousness is the alien righteousness of Christ, imputed to the believer and external to him, located within him, or in any way belonging to him.[1]

One must understand the Council of Trent to understand the present-day Roman Catholic view of justification. The dates for the Protestant Reformation are generally considered to be 1517-1648. The Council of Trent (1545-1563) was prompted by this Protestant Reformation and it has been described as the embodiment of the counter-reformation.

The English translation of the Council of Trent document by H. J. Schroeder[2] is considered by the Roman Catholic Church to be the accurate and authoritative translation of the Council's conclusions. In Schroeder's "Translator's Foreword," he clearly affirms the purposes for "Trent."

> In the list of general councils[3] Trent holds the first place, not only because of its r*estatement of Catholic doctrine* [emphasis mine] and its initiation of genuine reform, but also because of its extraordinary influence both within and without the Church.

Its purpose was twofold, to define the doctrines of the Church in reply to *the heresies of the Protestants,* [emphasis mine], and to bring about a thorough reform of the inner life of Christians … In … these dogmatic decisions … the council proclaimed to the world the doctrines that were committed to the keeping of the Church on the day of Pentecost. They are a sign erected on everlasting foundations indicating to the passer-by the straight road along which the Church has traveled ever since that day and along which she will continue to travel till the day of judgment. She recognizes no detours, for these lead only to destruction.[4]

A major purpose of the Council of Trent was to clarify and affirm the Roman Catholic view of justification in contrast to the presumed incorrect view by the Reformers. And these Council of Trent affirmations regarding justification are still the official doctrines of the Roman Catholic Church. One can trace their stated views following Vatican II (1962-65) as well as the *Catechism* (1995) and find no change regarding justification compared to the Council of Trent statements.

It's clear that their view of justification isn't the same as the normal evangelical understanding. Their system requires merit on the part of the participant, and justification is considered a process. In some of the Canons of Trent, the view of the Reformers is explicitly condemned.

Note well that each canon ends with "let him be anathema" which basically means let that person experience eternal condemnation. It is a very strong expression of desire by the drafters of the Trent document.

Here, for example, are four of the most important of them.

> Canon 9. If anyone says that the sinner is justified by faith alone, meaning that nothing else is required to cooperate in order to obtain the grace of justification, and that it is not in any way necessary that he be prepared and disposed by the action of his own will, let him be anathema.

> Canon 11. If anyone says that men are justified either by the sole imputation of the justice of Christ or by the sole remission of sins, to the exclusion of the grace and *the charity that is poured forth in the hearts by the Holy Ghost,* and remains in them, or also that the grace by which we are justified is only the good will of God, let him be anathema.

Canon 12. If anyone shall say that justifying faith is nothing else but confidence in divine mercy, which remits sins for Christ's sake, or that it is this confidence alone that justifies us, let him be anathema.

Canon 24. If anyone shall say that the justice received is not preserved and also not increased before God through good works, but that those works are merely the fruits and signs of justification obtained, but not the cause of its increase, let him be anathema.[5]

Note well the above statement "but not the cause of its increase." They are saying that good works increase our justification and our justification is dependent on good works. It seems clear they are declaring that justification is something that can increase—yes, it must increase along the journey to salvation. It is impossible to miss the intent and mood of these statements. And the fathers of the council knew full well what they were doing. "On June 21 Marcello Cervine (afterwards Pope Marcellus II) reminded them that no preceding council had dealt fully with this doctrine and that Luther's doctrine of justification by faith only was at the root of most of his errors on the sacraments, the power of the keys, indulgences and purgatory ... when in October a vote was taken on the question whether justification is inherent or imputed, the latter was rejected by a vote of 32 to 5. In other words, the Council opted for a transformationist view of justification."[6]

The transformationist view of justification means that this justification is a process throughout which increased righteousness is infused into the individual. Such a view leads to several obvious and serious questions. How much righteousness is needed to enter the presence of God for eternity? Is that amount of righteousness given instantly at some point in time? If so, what are all the conditions to be met to be given this amount of righteousness? How does one know when that amount of righteousness has been obtained? These are some of the questions for which the Roman Catholic view of justification provides insufficient answers.

No Roman Catholic person believing the justification theology of the Council of Trent could ever be certain of eternal salvation. According to Trent, assurance of salvation is impossible, for how can a person be sure of his salvation if this salvation depends on an inherent righteousness, which can be lost through deadly sins, and partly also because of the lack of the proper good works, which must accompany the grace given to him? In addition, a person claiming certainty about his or her eternal salvation condemns himself or herself by this very view.

And this is the view of most Roman Catholic people. I heard it repeatedly from the Roman Catholic people with whom I interacted in New Orleans.

IMPLICATIONS OF THEIR VIEW OF JUSTIFICATION

- Being right with God is a process with no certainty of ever completing the process.

- No Roman Catholic person can ever be certain he or she is right with God and therefore prepared for eternity.

- Confidence that one would experience heaven and not hell for eternity is not possible for the person believing in the Roman Catholic way of salvation

GRACE AND FAITH

Further, though the Roman Catholics will speak of salvation by grace, it is clear that for them grace means "merited favor" rather than unmerited favor. Therefore, they believe in "merited justification."

Note this declaration in the post-Vatican II 1995 *Catechism of the Catholic Church.*

> Moved by the Holy Spirit and by charity, *we can merit* [emphasis mine] for ourselves and for others the graces needed for our sanctification, for the increase of grace and charity, and for *the attainment of eternal life.* (Emphasis mine).[7]

To this day the Roman Catholic Church maintains that one cannot be justified by faith alone. Note this statement from Trent. "If anyone says that justifying faith is nothing else than confidence in divine mercy, which remits sins for Christ's sake, or that it is this confidence alone that justifies, let him be anathema."[8] "If anyone says that the sinner is justified by faith alone, meaning that nothing else is required to cooperate in order to obtain the grace of justification, let him be anathema."[9]

And note this statement from the *Catechism.*

> But faith apart from works is dead; when it is deprived of hope and love, faith does not fully unite the believer to Christ and does not make him a living member of his Body.[10]

> The disciple of Christ must not only keep the faith and live on it, but also profess it, confidently bear

witness to it and spread it … Service of and witness
to the faith are necessary for salvation.[11]

Clearly the Roman Catholic view of grace and faith are different
from the views of the apostle Paul. Repeatedly they make the point
that the terms *grace* and *faith* are not to exclude the concept of merit.
Clearly for them merit remains within the condition one must meet
to have eternal life.

WHAT ARE YOU THINKING NOW?

By now you likely understand the Roman Catholic official way of
salvation better than before. For some of you surprise may be your
response. Stunned may be the response of others.

Also you may wonder, and it is a good question, "just what does
the average Catholic person believe about the way to heaven?" Do
they typically believe the official Roman Catholic Church way of
salvation? Or do they believe something else?

In a Bible study I was conducting the well-informed visitor answered
with the following in response to the question regarding what she
might be trusting to get herself to heaven? Her answer: "I hope to get
to heaven, perhaps by way of purgatory, by faith plus good works."
It is almost certain that she verbalized this viewpoint because it is
consistent with the official Roman Catholic view and it is what she
hears regularly from the Roman Catholic priest.

I well remember the testimonies of dozens of people in New Orleans
who had been brought from what I believe to be the darkness of the
Roman Catholic system into the light of the word of God and the
liberating way of salvation message of the apostle Paul. Here is the
testimony of Cathy Puneky recorded in New Orleans in 2004.

Hello, my name is Cathy Puneky. I was raised in the church that taught that you could not go to Heaven with sin on your soul. And most of us we all spend a considerable amount of time in sinful activity. This was a major problem for us, and the church did not provide a clear-cut answer to how to deal with this problem. Jesus is our Savior but it also said that you had to go to church say certain prayers and do official good works in order to pay for our sins and gain Heaven; to get in good with God. I'll never forget the day it struck me as an adult that chances are I would never get around to really finding out what good works I needed to do, let alone have time to do them. I was busy. I had children and my fair share of selfishness. I didn't see myself as a bad person, but I judged myself according to other people. Even sometimes people who I thought may have done well enough, been good enough, done enough work to get to Heaven. I fell far short of the mark. The more I thought about it I now saw as so painful, so filled with sorrow, only to end with facing death and condemnation. I was wondering if others had ever been angry with God for leaving me (us) in such an impossible situation with no way out. Now I had children and I didn't know what to tell them. They were facing the same situation I was, and I couldn't help them. I began to wish that I had never been born, never had children, rather than face such an uncertain future with the possibility of hell.

And I had some friends who weren't angry or frightened and even in the face of sorrows and tragedies worse than I had gone through and they had a peace about them, even a joy. When I asked them about it they told me it was their faith in God their trust in Jesus that got them through, that gave them hope. I told them they were wrong because in my despair I was so frightened. But I began to want to have whatever they have and decided that I would look for it and I knew the Bible was a good place to start. Well, I went and visited a friend who had told me that she studied the Bible and I asked her for help, and she invited me to a Bible study at her home.

My husband and I went to this Bible Study, and I remember a lady asked why Jesus really had to die and we turned to the Bible for the answers. There we read Romans 3:23, "*all have sinned and fall short of the glory of God.*" And *Romans 6:23, "for the wages of sin is death,"* and *John 3:16 "for God so loved the world that he gave his only begotten son that whoever believes in him should not perish but have eternal life.*" And a very important one for me was Ephesians 2:8,9, "*for by Grace you have been saved through faith and that not of yourselves it is a gift of God: not as a result of works, that no one should boast.*" And finally, Romans 10:9," *that if you confess with your mouth Jesus is Lord and believe in your heart that God raised him from the dead you shall be saved.*"

It was like a light went on inside. It's as if I saw it in writing. Jesus paid the price that I couldn't. I could never do enough and it's a good God who doesn't allow his people to search in the darkness in fear and stumbling not knowing what to do. But He shows us. He wrote it in his Word. He paid the price himself. Well alone that night I studied the scriptures, and I made some decisions. I decided to stop arguing and complaining about it. I decided to believe that the Bible is the true word of God and I decided to tell God that his way was right not mine. I told Jesus I was choosing to believe that he paid the full price for our sins on the cross; that he rose from the dead showing that God accepted payment. All he asked of me was to trust him that he was able to do what He said he did, and He was able to pay the full price. I chose at that moment to stop all attempts at getting myself to heaven and trust in Jesus alone.

That was about sixteen years ago, and life is good. It still has its ups and downs. It's not perfect. I have my problems but I'm not alone. Jesus says he's always with me and I am no longer terrified of the future. I know my future is secure in Christ's hands. I know what to teach my children and I did. I still do good works and confess my sins. It's not to gain heaven but because this is what Jesus desires of me. I no longer see God as an angry judge waiting to destroy me, but I see him now as a loving father leading me and the peace and the joy that passes all understanding is mine now. I am truly free to love and serve God for who he truly is a good God who cares for sick and sinful people.

What are your thoughts and feelings about this testimony?

In a 1993 research project[12] I included the question: "While I was a Roman Catholic I believed" and the respondent was to answer yes to any of the questions that applied. Please contemplate the results. Think about the implications.

<u>Per Cent That Marked Yes</u>

Salvation is totally by grace	8
Salvation is by grace plus works	53
I believed in Jesus Christ as my savior	32
I was certain I would go to Heaven	19
Jesus Christ is the only way to heaven	15
Jesus Christ's death was necessary to enable me to go to Heaven	40
I would go to heaven, perhaps by way of Purgatory	76
I could go to heaven if I partook of the Eucharist regularly	48
Mary continues to help us get to Heaven	66
I became a Christian when I was baptized	59
If I died without mortal sin on my conscience I would go to Heaven or Purgatory	77
I would lose my right to Heaven if I committed murder	47
I would lose my right to Heaven if I stopped attending Mass	47

Note how purgatory was prominent in their thinking. For them purgatory is the place where additional payment can be made for their sins.

Also note the second highest number of participants answered, "Mary continues to help us get to Heaven." And only 40% believed that the death of Jesus Christ was necessary to enable them to go to Heaven.

Which of these responses are most surprising to you? Which helps you to better understand the thinking of the Catholic person? Which makes you want further clarification regarding just what your Catholic friend believes?

I hope you can now better understand when I assert, with good reason, that most Roman Catholic people do not understand the Bible-based way of salvation. Therefore, most of them need our love and effective attention, as enabled by God the Holy Spirit, to lead them to understand and respond to the saving gospel message.

A SUMMARY OF THE ROMAN CATHOLIC WAY OF SALVATION

<u>Authority</u> – They declare the scriptures to be the inspired Word of God.[13] However, in addition they believe authority is provided in/by:

> Apostolic Succession
> Tradition
> Hermeneutics (Interpretation of scripture)

<u>Sacraments</u> – They were established by Jesus Christ and there are seven of them, the most notable being baptism and the eucharist.[14] Partaking of the sacraments is required for salvation.[15] It is understood that as the priest pronounces the right words the recipient receives the grace benefits signified by the sacrament, such as forgiveness of sins and increased righteousness.

<u>Justification</u> – It is a process of infusion of righteousness as one participates in the sacraments. The Council of Trent document declares that justification is increased before God through good works.[16] The Council voted thirty two to five to reject the view that righteousness is imputed. Therefore, a practicing Roman Catholic can never know when he or she has enough righteousness to enter heaven.

<u>Grace</u> – To this day for them grace is understood to mean merited favor. "Moved by the Holy Spirit . . . we can merit . . . the graces needed for . . . the attainment of eternal life."[17]

<u>Faith</u> – In the Roman Catholic documents they repeatedly make the point that grace and faith are not to exclude the concept of merit. They even declare that a person who thinks he can have salvation by non-meritorious faith alone is to be cursed. "Let him be anathema."[18]

If they need salvation how can I help them?

Chapter 4
THE BIBLICAL WAY OF SALVATION

The first step toward helping your Roman Catholic friends is to be confident in your understanding of the biblical way of salvation.

I am writing this near unto Easter time. I am remembering the famous and loved hymn by Charles Wesley, *Christ the Lord Is Risen Today*. I get "goose bumps" even as I reflect on the words of this hymn. Some of my most treasured lines are:

> Love's redeeming work is done, Allelujah!
> Fought the fight, the battle won, Allelujah!
> Death in vain forbids him rise, Allelujah!
> Christ has opened paradise, Allelujah!
>
> Lives again our glorious king, Allelujah!
> Where O death, is now thy sting? Allelujah.
> Dying once he all doth save, Allelujah!
> Where's thy victory, O grave? Allelujah!

This hymn includes Wesley's reflections on portions of I Corinthians 15 where in verses 3 and 4 Paul declared:

> I delivered to you as of the first importance what I also received, that Christ died for our sins according

> to the Scriptures, and he was buried, and that He was
> raised on the third day according to the Scriptures,

The term "first" almost certainly here means first in rank or the chief in importance of all the important things I write. The core of the gospel that saves is the crucifixion and resurrection of Jesus Christ. One effective and final death for all sin. One victorious death to end the reign of death over all mankind.

Even though this hymn is so glorious and rings bells of joy and hope in my heart, of even greater importance is additional amplifying information we have from the hand of Paul's inspired written and infallible revelation.

I have been tempted to further simplify the following portions of this material. However, I believe each 'bit" of it is important for you to digest and understand. So please give it your good attention. It will be worth your time and mental investment.

Turn to <u>Paul's word in Galatians 1:6–9</u> to observe his key statements about the importance of the "right" gospel message. This passage is well known, usually well understood, and rarely disputed by serious-minded Bible believers.

In William Hendriksen's commentary on Galatians, his introductory remarks are worth repeating. "We have reached the place in the letter where ordinarily, according to the custom of the day, words of thanksgiving would be found. In Galatians, however, we are confronted with the very opposite. What we find *here* [Hendriksen emphasis] is not satisfaction but stupefaction: overwhelming amazement, painful perplexity … Paul could be stern. He was no flatterer … in Galatians *the very essence of the gospel* [Hendriksen emphasis] is at stake."[1]

I am amazed that you are so quickly deserting him who called you by the grace of Christ, for a different gospel; which is really not another; only there are some who are disturbing you and want to distort the gospel of Christ. But even if we, or an angel from heaven, should preach to you a gospel contrary to what we have preached to you, he is to be accursed! Or as we have said before, so I say again now, if any man is preaching to you a gospel contrary to what you received, he is to be accursed. (Galatians 1:6-9)

The major theme here is that there is one true gospel but also that there are "other of a different kind" of gospels that are described as "distorted," "perverted," or "corrupted." They aren't really a gospel message at all (v. 7) and are "contrary" to what Paul and those who minister with him, like Timothy, preach.

Furthermore, this distorted non-gospel message is so serious, disturbing, and destructive (non-saving) that anyone who would proclaim such a message is twice declared to be "accursed." *Accursed* is an almost unexpectedly strong word. It basically means "a man set apart for the direst of woes." In Romans 9:3 Paul used the term in the sense of separation from Christ and destruction for all eternity, which is the fate of the unsaved.

Plus, note that the verbal form associated with the term *accursed* could be more accurately translated "let him be." It is an imperative mood. It carries a forcible tone of command or a strong form of urgency or request. It adds the nuance that Paul is expressing a very strong desire that these gospel perverters experience an eternity of condemnation. Yes, this is the same Paul who so frequently championed the love, grace, and mercy of God. However, here he was declaring in the strongest terms that the pure and true gospel ought not to be distorted or perverted. The salvation of souls is at stake.

Paul was affirming that the gospel he had declared to them on previous missionary journey(s) was the gospel he had received from God by revelation (1:12). The gospel his words now reaffirmed in definition and clarification *is* the true gospel that saves. As a further amplification of Paul's certainty and seriousness, he declared that this true gospel shouldn't ever be changed. Paraphrasing 1:8 for amplification here is what he is saying. Even if I later in my ministry would speak a different kind of gospel, or even if a so-called heavenly sent messenger does so, or if any other of my associates, and probably by implication even if after my death anyone claims to come with apostolic authority and speaks a different kind of gospel, do not believe the messenger. And this is such a serious matter that I strongly wish that such gospel perverts be accursed, or eternally condemned.

Wow! This is it. This *is* the gospel. There is no other. Paul sounds like a theological heavyweight boxer engaging in the most important fight of his life.

Further Paul's communication is verse 9 could be paraphrased this way. "Therefore, I Paul again send this serious warning to you. 'Wolves' will come in among you and proclaim a non-saving gospel. Do not listen to them. Their error is so great that I strongly wish eternal condemnation for them."

Would you say Paul was serious about gospel accuracy?

Paul wrote with stunning absoluteness and certainty. Is there any question Paul meant that the gospel he received by revelation and included in holy scripture by the inspiration of God the Holy Spirit is the one gospel that saves?

This letter was written to combat deadly error that had infiltrated the churches in Galatia. The error was an attempt to pervert the true gospel of Christ (1:6–7; 3:1).

Who were these perverters, and why was Paul so concerned about their message? Some clearly advocated "self-works" as a means of securing salvation (3:13; 4:10, 21; 5:1, 4). These bearers of the deadly error were probably Judaizers from Jerusalem, who had accompanied or followed Peter (Acts 15:1).[2] F. F. Bruce states in *The Epistle to the Galatians that* the description of the perverters "agrees remarkably with Acts 15:1."[3] They likely were those who claimed an acceptance of the deity of Christ and salvation in Him but still believed one must be a convert to Judaism to be saved. Most believed salvation required some level of law keeping, along with faith (3:1, 11).

The above conclusions regarding the perverters of the gospel represent the most common understanding.[4]

This epistle was written to remedy a desperate situation in the early church. The purity of the gospel was at stake. The theme, *Christ liberates through the grace gospel*, provides the answer to deliverance from the penalty for sin for the unbeliever and from the power of sin for the believer. This theme unfolds as <u>the true gospel is *defended* in 1:11–2:21, *defined* in 3:1–4:31; and *practiced*, as exhorted in 5:1–6:15.</u>

While 3:1 marks the transition to the second major section of Galatians, where the definition of the gospel is amplified, Paul began this definition discussion in 2:15. In 2:11–21 he was defending the grace gospel in an encounter with Peter. "But when Cephas came to Antioch, I opposed him to his face, because he stood condemned" (2:11). Paul didn't fear Peter. He was convinced his gospel was received "through a revelation of Jesus Christ," rather than through some means of human ingenuity (1:11–12). Furthermore, he declared that he didn't consult with any human agency, church council, organization, or city as his source of authority (1:16–17).

In 2:11–16, he strongly asserted that safeguarding gospel purity requires exposing compromisers who fearfully capitulate to tradition. Some battles are worth fighting, and gospel purity is one of them.

Then in 15–16, he clarified the pure gospel. Even the most religious Jews need the same pure gospel (v. 15). In verse 16, one of the most important in the epistle, Paul states, "Nevertheless knowing that a man is not justified by the works of the Law but through faith in Christ Jesus, that we may be justified by faith in Christ, and not by works of the Law; since by the works of the Law shall no flesh be justified."[5]

First, note that Paul used the term *justified (dikaioo)* three times in this verse alone (eight times in Galatians).[6] Of the forty occurrences in the New Testament, twenty-seven appear in Paul's epistles. Paul "uses the word almost exclusively of God's judgment."[7] When used of men, it means "be acquitted, be pronounced and treated as righteous."[8]

For further understanding of Paul's meaning here, note four specific points. First, several statements are made about the recipients of the justification. All three usages of the term are in the passive voice, meaning the subject "receives the action." The subjects are "a man," in the sense of human beings versus non-human beings; "we" means Jews, though privileged above the Gentiles (even "we" Jews is the implication); and "no flesh" (of several meanings here, it means "a man of flesh and blood"[9]). The term *sarx* ("flesh"), when combined with *pasa,* as it is in this verse, means "every person, everyone."[10]

Therefore, every human being without exception, when faced with the judgment of God, if he or she is to be acquitted, must receive this pronouncement by someone other than himself or herself.

Second, it presupposes the need for acquittal or justification.

Third, note the three occurrences of the term "works of the Law." Any open-minded reader of the text quickly perceives the obvious; there is no law-keeping work that will secure or provide this acquittal.

Fourth, note that twice the text declares "faith in Christ"[11] as the condition necessary to appropriate this justification. Faith is from *pistis*. Faith includes the elements of intellectual content (knowledge of a fact), assent or the voluntary acceptance of the proposition as true, and *fiducia* or reliance and trust.[12] Therefore, this justification becomes ours by reliance and trust in the person and redemptive work of Christ. In 3:13 Paul declared, "Christ redeemed us from the curse of the Law, having become a curse for us."

Therefore, a careful interpretation of 2:16 requires the conclusion that for any man—Jew and Gentile and all human beings without exception—acquittal before the justice bar of God is provided in response to a reliance and trust in the person and redemptive work of Christ. Mankind appropriates this provision by faith alone. Absolutely no kind of law-keeping work is involved in the precondition for justification.

There is another related usage of the term *dikaioo*. Joseph Thayer makes this distinction. One meaning can be "to declare, pronounce, one to be just, righteous," and the other is "to show, exhibit ... one to be righteous."[13] The word has the former meaning in the Galatians passage. However, in James 2:21, the meaning is different. In James 2:14–26, James was discussing faith and works but was doing so to expose the "false claim of faith."[14] Tasker agrees when he says, "James now proceeds to demonstrate, where loving action is conspicuous by its absence, there is irrefutable evidence that real faith is lacking."[15]

James used the example of Abraham to support his argument. In Genesis 15:6, Abraham "believed God" and was therefore declared righteous or justified. Then in Genesis 22 (referenced in James 2:21) Abraham gave evidence of faith through his willingness to obediently sacrifice Isaac. James was arguing for "proof of faith … Works serve as a barometer of justification while faith is the basis for justification."[16]

He was answering the rhetorical question asked in verse 11, "Can that faith save him?" A faith that claims to be faith but doesn't demonstrate itself isn't saving faith. Abraham is an example of one who demonstrated his righteousness by obedient works.

Robert Pyne reaches this same conclusion. "What James is arguing is that believers are expected to demonstrate their faith through a changed lifestyle." He further states, "*We must not read the Pauline emphasis into James or Genesis, for they are not using the term with reference to a conversion, but with reference to the ongoing experience of the believer.*"[17]

In Galatians 3:1–14, Paul appealed to two lines of support for the correct gospel definition—experience in 1–5 and scripture in 6–14. If you wish to pursue Paul's argument in these portions, see my book *Roman Catholics: Saved or Lost?* [18]

Paul was saying in Galatians that Judaizing infiltrators and perverters of the gospel are a real threat to the gospel that liberates. He knew his gospel was the truth because he received it through revelation (1:12) and not from a manmade source. Neither tradition nor Peter scared Paul away from the truth.

Justification means to be declared righteous or to be acquitted before the judgment bar of God and is something accomplished totally outside any works by man. Any effort at justification by works will fail. The one condition for man to meet to appropriate God's provision through the redemptive work of Christ is faith, faith alone, and faith for any and all men everywhere. It is foolishness to believe anything else.

I feel confident in my understanding of Paul's meaning and intent in the above material in Galatians. I feel I am motivated to "get it right."

Now we will turn to <u>1 Corinthians 15</u> for what many believe to be the most concise and accurate summation of the gospel. Paul's intent in 1 Corinthians 15 is to "make known" (15:3) the most crucial aspects of the gospel message. "Christ died for our sins according to the scriptures … and that He was raised on the third day" (1 Corinthians 15:3–4). The gospel revolves around the death and resurrection of Jesus. It is news about specific (historical) events. Christ died. Christ arose. Based on the above study of Paul's understanding, this saving gospel must have an irreducible doctrinal content. The implications of Christ's death and resurrection are to be included in this understanding.

- The gospel is known to us by means of special revelation from God (1 Corinthians 2:7–10; Galatians 1:1–12), which is brought forth by the inspiration of God the Holy Spirit (2 Timothy 3:16). The holy scriptures provide for us a reliable and authoritative "word from God," which is our standard for faith and practice. This includes the true gospel (Colossians 1:5) that saves.

- It is Christ who died for our sins. This Christ is none other than the historical Jesus of Nazareth, who was God incarnate and is the unique and only God-man. He was born of the virgin Mary and lived a sinless life. He was resurrected from the dead, which points to His identity as indeed God; this fact points to the satisfaction of God's requirement for a justifying sacrifice, which demonstrates His victory over death as the capable giver of life, spiritual and eternal.

- Christ's death presupposes a needed solution for our sin problem, shared by all mankind, beginning at Adam's fall. Our sin should be understood as what falls short of God's holiness. The judgment for this sin, as established by God, the righteous judge, is eternal death, separation from God. We need a solution to this predicament. Also, even though there are psychological, environmental, and social implication of our sin, our "personal" sin is the primary problem.

- Christ dying "for" our sins has profound implications. The little Greek term *uper* ("for") has caused no small theological stir as to its meaning. However, when one interprets and correlates portions of scripture, such as Isaiah 53:4–6, 10; Matthew 20:28; John 1:29; 1 Peter 2:24; and 2 Corinthians 5:21, one concludes that the scriptures teach what is commonly called "penal substitution." The term penal means "relating to punishment" and substitution means "the act of taking the place of another." Jesus Christ has perfectly and completely accomplished such a substitutionary death. Do not confuse this with Roman Catholic penance.

- God, the ultimate judge, has found mankind wanting or lacking when compared to His holiness; thus, we are guilty and condemned. This condemnation includes temporal physical death and eternal spiritual death, separation from God. We individuals would face this penalty were it not for

God Himself providing in the person and death of Jesus Christ a satisfactory and sufficient "once for all" (Hebrews 9:26–28; 10:12) payment of the penalty "in our place." This substitutionary death propitiated the wrath of God (Romans 3:25; Hebrews 2:17), satisfying the demands of His justice.

- Just a cursory review of the forty uses of the Greek term *dikaioo* ("to justify") in the New Testament connects the concept of justification to the content of the gospel. In Galatians 2:16 alone the term is used three times. The term *justify* means to "be acquitted, or declared not guilty, be pronounced and treated as righteous."[19] The text presupposes that all mankind needs acquittal or justification. Furthermore, this justification occurs at the instant in time when one exercises saving faith in Christ. (Note the past tense in Roman 5:1.)

- Further, classic Christianity has understood that the "double imputation" indicated in 2 Corinthians 5:21 is part of the gospel content. The guilt and condemnation of mankind are transferred to Christ as our substitute when He "bore" or took this deserved judgment on Himself. Also, the alien to mankind, righteousness of Christ, is imputed to us so God can then declare us to be righteous, righteous indeed.

- Each individual must receive or appropriate this God-provided solution to the universal sin problem. Out of the good pleasure of His will, God initiated His lavish grace-filled deliverance package. On the cross Jesus Christ omnipotently declared, "It is finished" and died the death of all deaths. Then He rose from the dead. God sufficiently initiates His grace filled provision toward us to enable a saving response. To benefit from these provisions, we each must respond with non-meritorious faith. Accompanying this faith is spiritual regeneration by God, the Holy Spirit.

As additional help I include Pastor Steve Foster's sermon summarizing Romans 1-5.[20]

THE JUST SHALL LIVE BY FAITH

1. **ALL OF US HAVE SINNED AND HAVE FALLEN SHORT OF THE PERFECT RIGHTEOUSNESS OF GOD**

There is none righteous, no, not one (3:10 cf. Psalm 14:3).

- God has revealed His existence, power, and perfection to all people everywhere (1:18-20).

- Humanity, in general, has suppressed, resisted, and rejected the knowledge of God (1:21-23).

Even though *"the wrath of God is revealed from heaven . . ."* Romans 1:18.

> *God's wrath is His utter intolerance of whatever degrades and destroys. He hates iniquity as a mother hates the disease that would take the life of her child.* – A. W. Tozer.

- God has given over humanity to the pursuit of its own lusts, resulting in its own condemnation (1:24-32).

- The self-righteous moralist who condemns the sin of others while ignoring his own sin is also condemned (2:1-16).

- The religious person who relies on his outward "goodness" or religious rituals is also condemned (2:17-29).

- All people—regardless of ethnicity, social status, knowledge, or religion—are condemned in their sin (3:1-20).

2. **ALL OF US ARE SPIRITUALLY DEAD IN ADAM AND DESERVE ETERNAL DEATH BECAUSE OF OUR SIN.**

- Adam is both humanity's father and representative. Thus, His sin impacted us all with spiritual death (5:12).

- Our inherited spiritual death is confirmed by our own corrupted nature, individual sin, and physical death (5:13-21).

- Our two greatest enemies are sin and death. Thus, a true Savior must be able to conquer sin and death and give us life (5:12-21).

3. **ALL OF US NEED THE FREE GIFT OF JUSTIFICATION THRUGH THE DEATH AND RESURRECTION OF JESUS CHRIST.**

- Jesus Christ—the perfect Man and God in the flesh— died on the cross, in our place, as our righteous substitute for sin (3:25; 5:8).

- Jesus Christ, whose blood is of infinite value to atone for all of our sin, fully satisfied the wrath of God against sin (3:25; 5:18).

- Jesus Christ, the One with power over sin and death, is able to set us free from sin and death and give us new life (3:24; 5:17).

> *Justification is the act of God whereby He declares the believing sinner righteous in Christ on the basis of the finished work of Christ on the cross.*—Warren Wiersbe

4. **ALL OF US CAN BE DECLARED RIGHTEOUS BEFORE GOD BY FAITH ALONE IN JESUS CHRIST ALONE.**

*". . .(God is) just and the justifier of the one who has faith in Jesus" (*Romans 3:26).

As a "just" judge He required a sufficient payment for all sin of all time. Jesus Christ was that once for all sufficient payment.
(Note John 19:30; Hebrews 9:26-28; 10:10-12)

- Saving faith is putting one's full trust and reliance on Jesus Christ alone for one's salvation from sin and death (3:26).

- Saving faith excludes all self-reliance and boasting in one's own good works or outward obedience to the law (3:21-31).

The good news of the gospel is multi-faceted. Paul teaches us three important theological words regarding our salvation in Romans 3:21-31:

Justification. "An instantaneous legal act of God in which he (1) thinks of our sins as forgiven and Christ's righteousness as belonging to us, and (2) declares us to be righteous in his sight." (Grudem)

Propitiation. "The turning away of wrath by an offering, the placating or satisfying the wrath of God by the atoning sacrifice of Christ." (Ryrie)

Redemption. "The work of Christ on our behalf, whereby he purchases us, he ransoms us, at the price of his own life, securing our deliverance from the bondage and condemnation of sin." (Duncan).

- Saving faith has always been God's redemptive plan as exhibited in the examples of Abraham and David (4:1-25).

5. **ALL THOSE WHO TRUST IN JESUS CHIRST ARE RECONCILED TO GOD AND RECIPIENTS OF THE BLESSINGS OF SALVATION.**

- We have peace with God through our Lord Jesus Christ (5:1).

- We are surrounded by grace in Jesus Christ (5:2).

- We have real, sustaining hope in Jesus Christ (5:2-5).

- We are saturated with God's love in Jesus Christ (5:5-11).

    Nothing therefore should give greater joy to all of God's People than to meditate upon this love of Christ. Indeed, Our chief defect

> *as Christians is that we fail to realize Christ's
> love to us.* – D. Martyn Lloyd-Jones

- We are united with Jesus Christ—spiritually reborn into a new humanity, reigning in life, abounding in grace (5:15-21).

Note point 4 in Pastor Steve's notes. We are saved by <u>faith alone,</u> not faith plus some sort of meritorious work. Very important.

A Summary of Bible-Based Way of Salvation

<u>Authority</u> - The Bible, the Holy Scriptures, are understood to be the ultimate and final authority regarding salvation issues. It is considered to be a static, non-expandable foundation. There is no other authoritative revelation from God.

<u>Sacraments</u> - There are no sacraments in the sense that they are understood by the RCC. The term was not used by the apostles or Jesus Christ; it does not appear in our Bible. Jesus Christ did not establish the sacraments. Sacraments are not necessary for a person's salvation.

<u>Justification</u> - Justification means being declared innocent, not guilty. God can declare us so because the Cross work of Christ was fully sufficient to pay the full penalty for our sins. "It is finished" (John 19:30). We appropriate unto ourselves this justification by faith alone. At that point the righteousness of Christ is imputed, or credited, to our account.

<u>Grace</u> - Sourced in the immeasurable love of God salvation is provided to mankind as a free gift of superabounding grace. This is an unmerited grace not earned by keeping any set of moral laws or religious duty.

<u>Faith</u> - The necessity and benefits of salvation are appropriated or received by faith and faith alone. No self-works are required or even possible to earn this salvation.

Yes, it is clear that the Roman Catholic way of salvation is different from that defined in the authoritative and reliable holy scriptures.

Chapter 5
WHAT TO DO NOW?

PREPARE TO SOW THE SAVING GOSPEL SEED

By now you might be thinking that it is unlikely, or at least uncertain, that my Roman Catholic friends and acquaintances really do understand the saving gospel. So, what do I do?

My response: Prepare yourself so you can share with them the message of salvation provided by Jesus Christ. All of you can do so and there is likely no greater joy than to know that you have been used by God to aid your fellow man to escape hell and have heaven as his destiny.

I vividly remember the first time I shared the good news that saves with a person who responded positively. My hands were sweaty. This is important. Can I do it right? Obediently I shared, perhaps a bit clumsily. And somewhat surprisingly the person responded right away. And it was real as evidenced by his changed life. That was joy rarely matched by any other event in my life.

In the not too far distant past a popular song was meaningful to many in our church in New Orleans. After describing a scene in heaven where one meets several people with whom he had shared the gospel, the song concludes this way.

One by one they came
And I know up in heaven
You are not supposed to cry
But I am almost sure
There were tears in your eyes
And Jesus took your hand
He said my child look around you
For great is your reward

Can you think of the names of individuals who you would like to so greet you in heaven? It can be your thrilling experience!

I am very much aware that many of you, like many other believers, have the same fears and are reluctant to engage in personal evangelism. What kind of help would you like to overcome some of your felt needs when it comes to evangelism?

As a former pastor I feel deeply moved to be helpful to serious-minded saints who really wish to do what God wants. I prayerfully hope that the following material will indeed be helpful to you. It has been to many others.

The parable of the sower, soil, and seed in Matthew 13 is a good analogy in guiding us through this project. Prayerfully read Matthew 13:1–8 a couple of times.

Matthew 13:1–8:,

> 1. That day Jesus went out of the house and was sitting by the sea. 2. And large crowds gathered to Him, so He got into a boat and sat down, and the whole crowd was standing on the beach 3. And He spoke many things to them, in parables, saying 'Behold, the sower went out to sow; 4. and as he

sowed, some seeds fell beside the road, and the birds came and ate them up. 5. Others fell on the rocky places, where they did not have much soil; and immediately they sprang up, because they had no depth of soil. 6. But when the sun had risen, they were scorched; and because they had no root, they withered away. 7. Others fell among the thorns, and the thorns came up and choked them out. 8. And others fell on the good soil and yielded a crop, some a hundredfold, some sixty, and some thirty.

Clearly this is an agricultural analogy—a sower is sowing seed in soil. For us the sower represents the evangelist (intended to be every believer). The soil represents the heart of the unsaved person. The seed represents the gospel seed which is to be sown in the heart of the unbeliever.

It is my deep and sincere prayer as you pursue the following practical help material that God the Holy Spirit will enable you to apply it toward the salvation needs of many of your friends. What would bring you more joy and greater benefit to them?

THE SOWER NEEDS TO BE PREPARED TO SOW THE GOSPEL SEED

I suggest three basic starting places toward your preparation.

Recognize and accept <u>God's appointment</u> to be a gospel seed sower

In God's plan He has given each believer the privilege and the responsibility to take Christ and His gospel to individuals.

When you initiate a study of evangelism, I suggest you start with what is often called the Great Commission passages of Matthew 28:19–20 and Acts 1:8.

Prayerfully read and reread Matthew 28:19–20. "Go therefore and make disciples of all the nations, baptizing them in the name of the Father and the Son and the Holy Spirit, teaching them to observe all that I commanded you; and lo, I am with you always, even to the end of the age."

Most people understand the "go" to mean "by going," that is by taking the gospel to others, or by doing evangelism.

Prayerfully spend time meditating on Acts 1:8. "But you will receive power when the Holy Spirit has come upon you, and you will be My witnesses in Jerusalem, in all Judea and Samaria, and to the ends of the earth."

It has often been said that Acts 1:8 is the key that unlocks the door of Acts and the gates of Christian history. When in the life of Jesus Christ did He speak this portion? How does this timing relate to the importance or urgency of His words?

Acts 1:8 is our personal mandate, and some have suggested that every day of our lives needs to be spent under its ambition and authority. But in honesty I need to say that this is not always true for me. I have the same fears and reluctance that you may experience. We are walking this same pathway together.

What does this mean to you? How does this statement make you feel? What is the significance of Christ's phrase "My witnesses"? What is the significance that Christ mentions Jerusalem, Judea, Samaria, and the remotest part of the earth? As we pursue evangelism, how should we apply these geographical terms? Is there an application other than geographical? Could it provide a basis for reaching the people most like you and then spread toward those less like us? What does this mean to you personally and practically?

After the above study of Matthew 28:19–20 and Acts 1:8, each of you should be able to answer this question. Which view do you think is most consistent with Christ's intent?

> View 1: Evangelism is to be done by the "professionals."
> View 2: Evangelism is to be done by all believers.

Two portions of scripture continue to ring in my heart. "For whoever will call on the name of the Lord will be saved" (Romans 10:13). "How beautiful are the feet of those who bring good news of good things!" (Romans 10:15b). Think about it. Our God who is unsurpassed in greatness has passed on to each believer the opportunity to be a fruitful messenger of the gospel message that saves.

Have a **good balanced definition of evangelism**

In recent years there has been some debate among self-professed evangelicals regarding just what activity is to be included as God's evangelistic intent for us. Some have suggested that being an ambassador of reconciliation simply means we live out our faith in the web of relationships we already have.

However, I, and most evangelicals, believe it is to include both an appealing life in front of those who need Christ (I Peter 2:12) and also the verbalization of the gospel message. II Corinthians 5:17-21 is a central passage on this important topic.

17. Therefor if any man is in Christ, he is a new creature; the old things passed away; behold, new things have come. 18. Now all these things are from God, who reconciled us to Himself through Christ, and gave us the ministry of reconciliation, 19. namely, that God was in Christ reconciling the world to Himself, not counting their trespasses against them, and He has committed to us the word of reconciliation. 20. Therefore, we are ambassadors for Christ, as though God were entreating through us; we beg you on behalf of Christ, be reconciled to God. 21. He made Him who knew no sin to be sin on our behalf, that we might become the righteousness of God in Him.

Each of us is to be an ambassador for Christ (vs. 20) with the message about reconciliation (II Cor. 5:18-21). The term ambassador has the idea of a messenger, envoy, to be a person being sent by someone as a representative to speak a message for the sender. It is clear from this passage that this message is to be spoken by each believer and this message is the good news that God the Father was through Jesus Christ reconciling the world to Himself. And there is an appeal to hearers to respond.

So yes evangelism is to include speaking the gospel message that saves.

One more clarifying point will be helpful toward the overall goal of this project. Yes, evangelism can be thought of as the process of bringing good tidings, the gospel message. But sometimes the term *evangelism* is used narrowly only of the process of declaring, proclaiming, or presenting the gospel—what sometimes is called witnessing. However, at other times it is used of the entire process of relating and preparing the soil of the heart as well as the verbalization of the gospel. There is more than a hint of this in the sower, soil, and seed analogy. Also, when I did the 1993 research project, having relationships with authentic believers was an important step in the minds of the Roman Catholics who eventually trusted Christ as savior. Evangelism could also be thought of as including the post-conversion ministry that brings you, the evangelist, to a settled conviction of the salvation of the person as well as assurance of salvation by the person, a portion of the ministry called "preserving the fruit" discussed later in this book.

This entire process—that is, a broader definition—will be considered "evangelism" for the purposes of this presentation. Do you understand? Why is this an important point to make here?

It is important that we understand that evangelism is more like farming than selling. It's a process more than an event.

What are some of the implications of this statement?

Helpful attitudes are important

A positive attitude is needed as we pursue what seems like a difficult task, yes, even impossible if we attempt it in the energy of our own flesh or mere human wisdom and determination.

Remember our <u>power source</u>. Our principal enemies are Satan and his host of deputies (Ephesians 6:11–12). We understand this force to be the fallen angels, sometimes called demons (Matthew 12:24; 1 Corinthians 10:20; James 2:19; Revelation 9:20).

Particularly note Matthew 12:24 and Ephesians 6:11–12. How do these passages support the idea that Satan has these unseen "principalities and powers" who are willing to do his bidding?

Today some people, even professing Christians, wish to deny the existence of Satan.

However, we need to focus on the God-provided supernatural power source, God the Holy Spirit. Note passages like Galatians 5:16; Ephesians 5:18; John 16:8–11; and Titus 3:5.

Each believer has available to him or her all the supernatural enablement needed to do his or her part in the evangelistic process. Therefore, we can go forth prayerfully, dependently, and confidently. Remember, we cannot convert anyone; nor are we responsible to do so. We should lovingly and effectively take Christ and the gospel to lost and needy people, but only God does the saving work.

Most likely most of us don't yet have the kind of compassion we need toward lost people. I am certain I don't. Read, reread, and meditate on Matthew 9:36. "And seeing the multitude, He felt compassion for them, because they were distressed and downcast like sheep without a shepherd."

What do you sense was in the heart of the God-man Jesus Christ?

He saw the multitudes as sheep the shepherd had abandoned, as those who were perishing on the barren, wind-swept plain. He "felt, had pity" for them. What do you suppose this felt like?

Though I have far to grow in this area, a couple of exercises have helped. First, meditate on the reality of hell and eternal condemnation of each and every "lost" person. Caution: This exercise can sometimes be overwhelming, so be careful. Don't spend too much time doing it. Second, as you go through life and see people going to and fro, occasionally try to think of them as spiritually dead people (not all will be) with a great need.

When we consider evangelism, another important attitude we should have is that of <u>obedience.</u>

Obedience for the believer has been defined as keeping God's commandments as our outward indication of inward health and love for Christ (John 14:21). "He who has My commandments and keeps them, he it is who loves Me; and he who loves Me shall by loved by My Father, and I will love him, and will disclose Myself to him." Engaging in the process of evangelism is one of those Christian practices that we each are intended to do. And the motivation to do so is found in our mutual love relationship with Jesus Christ.

Doesn't God the Father love all believers? What does the text mean when it says, "He who loves Me [demonstrated by obedience] will be loved by My Father"? I understand the verse to include something that has been called the cyclical process in our Christian life experience. As I increasingly love God the Father, demonstrated by my obedience, He will further enlighten my mind to the magnitude of his love for me. And Jesus Christ will open the veil so we can grasp more deeply His unmatched love for me. I think this deserves the occasional WOW!

Yes, we can go deeper and deeper into the heart of God. Think about the personal benefit of engaging in the evangelism process. You will be most pleased you have chosen to do so.

As we have indicated, clearly God our Father and the Lord Jesus Christ, our Savior and Head of His body, the church, wants and commands us each to be obedient in personal evangelism.

THE SOWER NEEDS TO PREPARE THE SOIL OF THE LOST PERSON'S HEART

Some aggressive evangelistically minded persons will almost immediately begin to bombard people with the gospel using the same methodology and approach with everyone. In chapter six I provide what has been to many people practical help toward being able to sow the gospel seed.

This includes giving good attention to preparing the soil of the lost person's heart through relationship development with them. They will be able to sense whether or not you care for them as a person.

We can also prepare the soil by validating the authenticity of the Christian message by the way we live our lives. Powerful indeed.

It is important to understand that each person is unique and that different methods may be required for different people. Eventually they need to hear the clear gospel message.

THE SOWER, OR SOMEONE ELSE, NEEDS TO HARVEST THE FRUIT

Some of you will feel confident enough to pursue sharing the gospel with your friends. If this describes you and if the person is willing for you to allow it, prayerfully do so. Keep in mind the importance of the ministry of the Holy Spirit. Every conversion to saving faith in Christ is enabled by God the Holy Spirit.

For those of you who feel a need for help see a clear gospel presentation this help is included in chapter eight

Others of you may not yet feel confident in sharing the gospel or may not be convinced it is what God intends that you do. And others may be thinking that you need lots of help or training in this area. Help for you is the main content of chapters six and seven.

A CONCLUDING WORD TO THIS CHAPTER

At this point you might be tempted to give a quick look at the remaining portions of this book and quickly conclude that it is too much, or perhaps you feel even unnecessary, for you to seriously consider.

Notes like the following from Beth Terry convince me otherwise.

> Pastor Larry and Mrs. Marcella, as you know my Mom, Mary Anne Cuadrado, was given eyes to see after all those years of being a staunch Catholic. She

told my sister she no longer believed in purgatory. I cannot tell you how many masses she purchased and candles she lit on behalf of departed souls.

She assured me she knew that Jesus paid it all and believed this was true. She knew her sins were forgiven and nothing could grasp her out of the hands of our Lord. She passed into glory this past Wednesday. I was with her, I prayed over her, and sang "Jesus Loves Me" in her last moments.

As she entered this last medical crisis my prayer was for God to direct my steps, but as I replayed the events as they unfolded, I see, even when I tried to take my own direction, the Lord orchestrated these last days of her life. Our God is Sovereign!
She was a blessing to many but I am blessed to have known her as Mom. Thank you for your ministry in our lives, and particularly to Catholics. I have filed many things you have taught me and your wisdom serves me well.

After I requested Beth's permission to include the above in this book, she responded with the following.

Dear Pastor Miller, I am honored to have you share my Mom's road to salvation in your book. Your love and perseverance in reaching Catholics with the truth of the Gospel message is evident. I know my parents sat in programs at Berean over the years and I know seeds were planted.

It seems that we have never heard of such spiritual struggles as we are hearing in these days. Recently when Pastor Steve unfolded Romans 8, I rested in God's truth.

Either we believe God's Word or we don't. Yes, a believer became an overcomer through the blood of the Lamb. I am in awe. We all are miracles, recipients of God's grace and only righteous through the blood of Jesus Christ.

Thank you for realizing the truth behind Mom's struggle. May your readers each be graced through your book. Love to you and Mrs. Marcella.

So yes, pursue loving your Roman Catholic friends and family members well!

Chapter 6

PREPARE THE SOIL BY ENGAGING THE LOST PERSON

Relax, I do not suggest that you start blasting the Roman Catholics or become so aggressive that you turn them away from interest.

So how does one become a more effective evangelist for the benefit of one's friends and others who need salvation?

In today's world it is increasingly clear that we need to know something about the mindset of the person we are attempting to evangelize. For you who are interested in effective evangelism of those with different worldviews, I recommend to you missionaries Danny and Becky Loe, dannydloe@gmail.com; Ratio Christi, ratiochristi.org; and Southeastern Evangelical Seminary, ses.edu.

In this project we are focusing on evangelizing lost Roman Catholics. My starting assumption is that most of them have a Christian theism worldview. This means they likely believe God is there, that is they are not atheists. He is our source of authority for what is true and what is good or morally right and we each are accountable to Him as our ultimate judge. We are created in God's image therefore each individual has significance, purpose and value. Jesus Christ has an important role in determining our eternal destiny. This gives you an idea of what most of your friends likely believe, at least to some degree. You can usually start with this assumption. If you find otherwise you can connect with one of the sources mentioned above.

As I introduce what is to follow in the next chapters, remember this core issue: our evangelism efforts must be centered on the absolute necessity of the ministry of the members of the Godhead –to illumine or enlighten (John 1:5; 2 Corinthians 4:4, 6; Acts 26:18[1]), to convict or convince (John 16:7–11[2]), and to regenerate (Titus 3:5[3]).

THROUGH PREPARATION OF THE SOIL OF THE HEART OF THE UNSAVED PERSON

For those readers who are accustomed to thinking evangelism equals proclaiming the gospel message or are inclined to focus almost entirely on "harvest," this material may feel unnecessarily slow. And on some occasions that might in fact be the case. If you are privileged to meet someone who understands the gospel and is ready to respond with a saving faith, certainly help them to do so. However, please keep in mind that my approach to defining evangelism is also legitimate, and I, as well as many others, have experienced a process like what we propose here, with good success and solid converts. Furthermore, with certain kinds of people—many Roman Catholics, for example—it has often proved to be better than the "quick harvest" approach. Yes, it requires patience, and yes, it takes effort.

Most likely you will never need to utilize everything in chapters six – eight. However, you may get "stuck" at some point in your approach toward your unsaved friend. You can utilize the portion of the following material that meets the need at that point.

Example 1:   See my story later in this chapter about interaction with the attorney.

Example 2:   In chapter seven I have a section that can be helpful in establishing why we can trust the Bible. Perhaps all of this is not needed because the person might already have confidence in the Bible or time might not permit going through all of it. Or perhaps only some of it is needed. If so use it.

Example 3:   I am convinced that helping the person understand the sufficiency of the cross work of Christ IS important. In chapter seven I have a couple of pages summarizing the teaching on the "once for all" death of Christ in Hebrews chapters nine and ten. Use it only if needed but it is there in case this becomes a crucial point for the person to understand.

Enough examples. Think you understand the point.

UNDERSTAND THE KIND OF SOIL WE ARE CULTIVATING

For those who are now engaged in some sort of agricultural business or have an agricultural background, this point is well understood. For others the point is easily discerned. The soil on the hillsides of mountainous regions is different from the soil on the plains of another region. Soil is different in different countries and different in the regions of the same country. And so forth.

It's likewise extremely important to understand the kind of soil, or mindset, of the typical Roman Catholic person.

It is important that you understand such issues as religious background and worldview of the person you are attempting to evangelize. In chapters two and three, I included a portion of material from the Roman Catholic official documents on such key topics as authority, sacramentalism, and justification. I urge you to review it at this point. It is greatly helpful to you the evangelist to have a sufficient grasp of these issues as you move further into the process with unsaved Roman Catholics.

CULTIVATING THE SOIL OF THE LOST PERSON'S HEART

Cultivating the Soil of the Lost Roman Catholic Person's Heart through Relationship Development

How might we do this? Based on the 1993 South Louisiana Survey and our own experience, it is very important that someone the person knows and trusts is perceived to love him or her. Learn to be sensitive to the person's interests and attitudes. Pray for the person and spend time with him or her. Enter the person's world.

A common kind of statement made by the responders to the 1993 survey went something like this: "A friend showed concern in a time of need."

Does this make sense? What else have you found to be helpful? What other comments do you think the people that you know would make?

A premature confrontation may create seed-sowing barriers. Early in this process, confrontation and argumentation often increase resistance.

Influence is often effective when the person wants your influence. Learn to be sensitive to the person's interest and attitude. Many Roman Catholic people have a strong prejudice against Protestants.

Their conscience may often make it difficult to discuss religion with you.

Therefore, spend much time in prayer and relationship development. Do it!

Cultivating the Soil of the Lost Roman Catholic Person's Heart through Affirmation of the Christian Message

How might you do this?

The witness of life is undeniable and powerful. Often our lives speak more loudly than our words. While we need to get around to actually verbalizing the gospel, don't underestimate the importance and power of affirming the message through lifestyle.

Note the words of Peter in 1 Peter 2:12. "Keep your behavior excellent among the Gentiles, so that in the thing in which they slander you as evildoers, they may because of your good deeds, as they observe them, glorify God in the day of visitation."

I agree with a common understanding that the "day of visitation" refers to the second coming of Jesus Christ. The implication would be that as the Gentiles (think today's unbelievers) observe your lives, they will become believers, thus glorifying God when Christ returns.

"This brief section (I Peter 2:11,12) sketches Peter's 'battle plan' for the inevitable confrontation between Christians and Roman Society."[4]

Note well this real historical happening that well demonstrates the importance of affirming the Christian message.

Eileen arrived at our church in New Orleans in the mid 1980's, brought there by her former college roommate. Eileen had just gone through a divorce and had three children, ages 8, 10, 12. Eileen was devastated and overwhelmed. Her friend eventually took Eileen to one of our Ladies Bible Studies on the Epistle to the Romans. Eventually Eileen understood the gospel and trusted Jesus Christ as her Savior, as did each of her three children. Her story is an amazing one. Each of those children are now married with children of their own and all three, along with their spouses, are engaged in full time vocational Christian ministry—two of them missionaries and the other a church planting pastor in New Orleans. Here is a very interesting part of her story. After attending her first study in Romans, Eileen commented about how she was so impressed. When I heard this I automatically thought, she must have been impressed with the teaching skill of the lady leading the study or some aspect of the powerful content of Romans, both of which would have been impressive. But, no, what impressed her most was the lives and interactions of the women in the study. I love this story, repeated by several women who were in the Bible Study.

Why is this word about Eileen included here? Does it make sense to you?

As I write this book, I periodically pause, remembering specific people and events, such as Eileen's experience. Even to this day, joy floods my heart.

The credibility of the church corporately in the community is important.

The credibility of a particular local church or a group of churches, say like a denomination, depends largely on the observed lives of those who are part of it. Sincerity of convictions, a Christlike lifestyle, and carrying attitudes are hugely important.

Also, a particular church may have a "corporate" reputation. When discussing this concept with pastors and church leaders in Eastern Europe, I asked for their responses. One pastor indicated that in his town he would occasionally get a phone call from a businessman looking for a new employee. He asked whether the pastor knew of any men wanting a job. The people from this congregation were known for being honest and hardworking.

What examples can you think of?

BE PREPARED WITH RIGHT (MOST PRODUCTIVE) METHODOLOGICAL AIM

Methodologies

Sometimes people think there is one and only one way to evangelize. Sometimes people are inclined to evangelize every person by the same methodology.

Do you see any problems with this approach to evangelizing? If so, what are they?

Most of us have experienced people responding with all sorts of different approaches to presenting the gospel. However, we also know methodology is important. We should be aware of such and want to be good stewards of what God has given us to do. As an example, note the approach by Jesus Christ in John 3 compared to His approach in John 4. Read the account of Jesus with Nicodemus and Jesus with the Samaritan woman. Look at the differences in his approach with each. Briefly describe the different methods used.

We need to be aware of the mindset of the person(s) we are evangelizing so as to apply the most appropriate methodology. In this case we need to understand the mindset of the Roman Catholic person. We will say more about this in material to follow.

This issue may be a bit controversial, but based on my experience and research, I believe there is validity to the following, so please give it consideration.

Generally *ineffective* methodologies include these two.

The first of two ineffective methodologies are what could be called the "confrontation or decision-oriented approach." Does this come as a surprise to you?

Why or why not?

What words might describe what has been called the "confrontation or decision-oriented approach"?

What additional thoughts do you have about this point?

If in a group discuss it.

The second ineffective methodology is what could be called the "blast the Catholics method." A former Roman Catholic priest came to our church in New Orleans. We advertised it as an evangelistic outreach event. One young lady in our congregation invited her mom to attend. The former Roman Catholic priest was very angry at the Catholic Church and basically ridiculed anyone who was Roman Catholic. This young ladies' mom left in tears and became more devoted to the Catholic Church.

Is this a valid illustration of the point that the "blast the Catholics method" is (at least usually) ineffective?

During one of the seminars I did in Eastern Europe, I chose to ask the participants whether the material was beneficial to them in their evangelistic effort. I had traveled six thousand miles and spent considerable dollars to get there. I didn't want to waste money, my time, or their time. Several men said it was indeed helpful. One man, whom we will call George, gave this testimony. He had been working at church planting in a nearby village. His former approach had been to argue with the Orthodox about which group was right. There was basically no fruit. After attending the first couple of seminars, he changed his methodology to more like what we describe here, and he had seen two converts during recent months.

Does this make sense to you? Why or why not?

We will include two generally effective methodologies.

The first effective method is what can be called "informational evangelism." Our experience is that the lost person has a lot of relearning or informational input needed. There are several different ways this can be done. One of the methodologies we found effective was to conduct what could be called a four-week discovery series. Someone would invite his or her friends or neighbors to the person's home for four consecutive weeks. It would be a relaxed atmosphere with dessert and coffee. The guests could ask me any question they might have about religion, spirituality, or the Bible. The questions included might be these and others:

How do you know God exists?

How do you know you can trust the Bible?

What happens to those who have never heard of Jesus?

Why did Jesus need to die anyway?

How can you be certain you are going to heaven?

There are numerous other ways to engage in such a manner with the unsaved Roman Catholic person(s). What are some you can think of?

Paul spoke of apologetics in Philippians 1:16 (Greek word *apologia* means "defense or speech"). The verb form means "to speak so as to absolve oneself, to defend oneself, to justify myself in one's eyes." Peter also exhorted us in 1 Peter 3:15, "Always being ready to make a defense [same term] to everyone who asks you to give an account for the hope that is in you, yet with gentleness and reverence." It seems that we need to be prepared to listen to and answer honest-searching questions.

We found that even after many of them got involved in the Bible (reading it, hearing it taught, and so forth), from three months to three years were required for them to adequately understand the biblical-grace gospel. Remember, when we discussed the issue of "understanding" in Matthew 13 there was a huge difference in understanding between the hearer who responded to the saving gospel message and the person who didn't.

Don't assume they understand terms and concepts adequately. One lady said that each Sunday she repeated, "Jesus was crucified and on the third day rose from the dead." But she didn't understand what this was supposed to mean to her personally. Be prayerful and patient and give them the information they will surely need.

Do you understand the importance of this issue? Does it make sense that we include it in this project? Why or why not?

The <u>second effective method we will include here is what can be called "Bible-centered evangelism."</u>

Much of the information needed as per above will be in the Bible and from the Bible. But it is very important that the person you are evangelizing gets engaged with the Bible itself. The holy scriptures are powerful as they are planted into a person's heart and as what they hear or read is illuminated by God, the Holy Spirit. Remember the words of Hebrews 4:12. "For the word of God is living and active and sharper than any two-edged sword and piercing as far as the division of soul and spirit, of both the joints and marrow, and able to judge the thoughts and intentions of the heart." The concepts of "joints and marrow" and "soul and spirit" here probably mean something like the word pierces to the depth of the "soul and spirit," which stand for the innermost factors of our immaterial nature, just as the "joints and marrow" stand for the material aspect of our existence. The verse certainly indicates the power of the living holy word of God.

Study 1 Peter 1:23–25. Record here as many different statements as you can find about the "word of God."

When you get to the seed-sowing phase of the evangelistic effort, get them into the Bible. Reading the Bible, hearing it taught, being engaged in a group Bible study—by whatever means attempt to get the interested person under the influence of the holy scriptures. One way is to meet with him or her personally and study, giving him or her opportunity to ask questions.

Get them into the Bible. There will be more about how to do this in chapter seven.

MINI DECISIONS DURING THE CULTIVATION PHASE

Be aware of where they are in their thinking and feeling. As the person progresses toward readiness for the seed-sowing phase, he or she will often make several mini decisions. Below are some of the probable points through which the person may progress. I have found it to be very helpful to be ministering to the person "where he or she is" in his or her thinking. This may be the implication in Colossians 4:4, "that I might make it clear in the way I ought to speak," A summary of the Colossians 4:2-6 passage is included as Appendix B.

Note the following material regarding "decision points" or "mini decisions." This is more important than many have been inclined to think. Numbers of students of evangelism and missions' methodology have written about the "decision points" people usually move through toward accepting the Christ of the Bible and the grace gospel message. Sometimes this is in the context of how far away they are culturally and religiously from the biblical gospel. As an example, a Muslim person doesn't believe in the Trinity; therefore, he or she is farther away on this point than the Roman Catholic person who does, at least theoretically, believe in the Trinity.

I have identified numbers of decisions people may make along the way toward understanding the biblical grace gospel and responding to Jesus Christ with saving faith. Some people go through all these decision points, and others may skip over some of them. It has been extremely helpful to understand just where the person is as you seek to evangelize and minister to him or her "where he or she is" rather than where you might want him or her to be. Does this make sense? Discuss?

Now the mini decisions:

1. Being aware that something has happened to the messenger or that the messenger is different
2. Asking questions why he or she is so different
3. Being aware and admitting I have a need that isn't satisfied or admitting that everything isn't okay
4. Believing the messenger is in a cult or is a religious fanatic
5. Trying to tell me my church is wrong (I am angry)
6. Trying to convert me (this makes me stay away)
7. This thing with my friend isn't just a passing thing. It seems to be lasting.
8. Noticing a desirable quality of life he or she lives with peace and confidence
9. Realizing he or she seems to rely a great deal on the Bible
10. Understanding there are answers that are in the Bible
11. Thinking I would like to know more about the Bible
12. And there may be others.

Do you understand what this list is about? If you are in a group discuss.

I was at an attorney's office, taken there by a friend. We were there to prepare incorporation papers for a new ministry organization. My friend received a phone call that required him to leave the office for some time. While he was away, the attorney indicated in some manner that he was struggling with where he could find truth as it related to religion. Having gone through a similar experience in my early twenties, I began to share my story and how I came to be convinced I could trust the Bible. He became engaged with me with some interest. As my friend returned, he heard a bit of the conversation and later asked me what was happening. My friend had been trying to witness to this attorney for quite some time, with little to no outward success. I indicated that perhaps I had discovered (from my part it seemed accidental) where "he was at" in his thinking, and even though my friend had been "witnessing," the attorney wasn't there yet and ready to listen. Anyway, it certainly seems that the above list is the way it happens for a lot of people.

What do you think about it? Does it make sense to you? Discuss.

What would you add to or remove from the list of decision points?

Make a list of five people you know whom you believe to be lost. Try to identify where you think they are along the way in this decision process.

Names	Where Are They in the Decision Process?
_____	_____

_____   _____

_____   _____

_____   _____

_____   _____

How might a person be moved from stage to stage or one decision point to the next?

Each person is different, but keep in mind the weapons in your arsenal.

- You have *light* to shine into his heart (John 1:9; Matthew 5:14, 16).

- The Holy Spirit provides the supernatural power to accomplish conviction (John 16:8,9) and regeneration (Titus 3:5).

- And you have the sword that can strike deep into the understanding of the unsaved person: the Word of God (Ephesians 6:17; Hebrews 4:12).

- And prayer is a key weapon (Colossians 4:2–3).

Using effective methodology is important, but we *must* remember that the battle over a soul is a supernatural one.

Review the material in this chapter six. Pay particular attention to these sections:

Cultivating the Soil of the Lost Person's Heart

Be Prepared with Right Methodology

Mini Decisions during the Cultivation Phase

Were any of the thoughts in these sections new to you? Which of the sections contained material that was helpful to you? What was it? Why was it helpful?

Other thoughts?

If you are in a group discuss with them.

Chapter 7
SOW THE GOSPEL SEED

I am convinced that the material regarding preparing or cultivating the soil of a lost person's heart is very important to the successful evangelization of lost Roman Catholic people.

At some time, the earliest point at which the listener is open to hear, the seed should be sown, or the gospel should be verbalized.

I have here included several ideas that have been helpful at one time or another and with certain people in this seed sowing process. It is not to imply that all of it must be used with each individual. Each person or situation is different. You can prayerfully pick and choose which parts of the following are helpful in your situation.

TRANSITION FROM CULTIVATING TO SEED SOWING

Often there is tension here. For me personally it is one of my greater obstacles in the God-intended evangelism process. We might be fearful that we may be moving too quickly, the person might not be prepared, or might lose a friend. But we are sensing that if we really love the person, we ought to move toward verbalizing the gospel. And we do want to be faithful.

Some helpful suggestions:

- Don't allow self-centeredness in the form of fear or loss prevent you from lovingly making this transition.

- Remember that the most loving thing you can do for the person is to introduce him or her to the gospel with clarity.

- Listen well for comments such as the following:

    "You seem to handle problems well."
    "Why do you train your children in such a fashion?"
    "Why is your church so important to you?"
    "How did you get to know so much about the Bible?"
    "You seem certain of your destiny."
    "What else would you add?"

- When such questions are asked, certainly answer the question asked and point to Jesus Christ as your Savior and enabler, and the Bible as your source for principles that work in life.

- What should you do if the person doesn't provide such an opening kind of question?

    o Pray for an opportunity.
    o Choose to test the soil to take the conversation toward the seed-sowing level by asking such questions as the following:

    "Have you ever wondered about your eternal destiny?"
    "Are you certain of your destiny?"
    "Would you like to know for certain you will go to heaven when you die?"

"Have you wondered what the Bible says about
_____ [any number of options that might be
of interest to the individual]?"
"Do you have any questions in your mind about religion?"

What have you found helpful?

Do these "transition" suggestions make sense to you? What would
you remove from the list? What would you add?

Sometimes there are encounters with individuals with whom you
don't have a relationship. Pray and quickly discern their level of
understanding and preparedness to receive the gospel. In these
encounters a right objective might be to help them at least take the
next step toward and, if possible, all the way to conversion. Aim to
share the gospel with them, if possible—that is, if the door of their
heart is open.

GET THEM INTO THE BIBLE

Good seed, good harvest. At this point the Bible becomes the focus.
The word of God, the Bible, is extremely important in the evangelizing
process. It is our authority for what to believe. The Bible also has a
special supernatural ability to affect people at the deepest part of their
being. Spend time prayerfully reading and rereading Hebrews 4:12.
"For the word of God is living and active and sharper than any two-
edged sword and piercing as far as the division of soul and spirit, of both
joints and marrow, and able to judge the thoughts and intentions of the
heart." What does this verse say that relates to our topic of evangelism?

Note this important point regarding something that needs to be done with sensitivity. Encourage them to use their own Bibles if they have one. And be very cautious. Don't embarrass them regarding what they don't know about the Bible. The Roman Catholic Bible the person may have is likely a good translation.

If others are willing to read the scripture in their own Bible, then encourage them to do this. If not, you could read in your Bible with them following along in their Bible. As you start asking them questions about what some particular portion means, again encourage them to focus on the text in their own Bible. At least move as far in this direction as possible. Some people may want to listen to you read your Bible, and at this point many of them will trust that you are reading what it actually says.

Point: Encourage them to interact with the text in their own Bibles but don't be overly pushy. You want them to be as comfortable as possible with the circumstances of the interaction. I remember my early days of being an adult Christian and lacking good Bible use skills. I would have been embarrassed if a more seasoned believer had asked me to read something from, say, Nehemiah. I would have been a bit challenged to quickly find it.

SUGGESTIONS FOR TRANSITIONING INTO THE BIBLE

1. *The Bible speaks to a problem or need.* The most common denominator with the largest percentage of people is the area of felt needs. Begin here. Assess some specific sensitive area of need. It could be a struggle with child-rearing, fear of the future, fear of loss of love, fear of failure, financial struggles, frustrations with national politics and economic circumstance, doubts about eternity, an agnostic bent, and so forth. Suggest that the Bible has something to say about

this area of concern and give certain passages to read and then get back together to discuss.

2. *Encourage the person to read the Bible.* If he or she will read the Bible regularly, the light will shine into the heart of darkness, and questions will arise in the mind. Today many Roman Catholics own a Bible. If they don't, offer to get them one and get them a Roman Catholic translation if they prefer.

3. Some thought starters might be helpful, such as:

    •   "Did you know that St. Peter's description of the end of the world sounds like an atomic explosion?" Then lead him or her to Second Peter 3:10–13.
    •   "Do you know why the Jews and Arabs are still fighting today?" Point the person to the story of Isaac and Ishmael in Genesis 16 and 21.
    •   "Did you know the Bible describes the conditions in the world in the last days?" See Second Timothy 3:1–5 and others.
    •   "Would you like to better understand what God has to say about family issues, abortion, capital punishment, finances, and so forth?" Usually something can be found that will interest the person.

        What would you add?

4. Meet people on their ground. Start them at their level of understanding and opinions, no matter how wrong or immature they are. I didn't say to agree with these

wrong opinions. Be sensitive to the individual's social and psychological pressure. Try to meet the person at a neutral site if possible. He or she may not be ready to let his or her friends, family, or neighbors know the person is involved in a Bible study with a non-Roman Catholic person.

5. *Stick to the basics.* Right away there is a temptation to debate issues like Mary, birth control, or saints. However, the goal is the salvation of the needy person, not a victory in a debate. Emphasize the truths of authority and biblical grace salvation.

6. *Do not obscure the message.* Be careful not to include your own convictions about such things as "entertainment choices" or "alcohol drinking at a wedding" or _____. These lesser- important issues might derail the conversation from what's more important. Stick to the basics *of authority and salvation.* And do not feel you must expound on all you know about salvation truth, such as election or predestination, the kind of glorified bodies we will have, or our reign with Christ in eternity. If they ask questions about these issues, give a briefer kind of answer and try to get back to the more basic issues as soon as possible.

Do the above suggestions for transitioning into the Bible make sense? What would you remove from or add to the list?

ESTABLISH THE AUTHORITY OF THE BIBLE

Please do not overlook the importance of doing this. A person's basis for authority is extremely important. Why is this true?

Typical Roman Catholic people lean heavily on tradition and what their priest says. However, you could show them that the Roman Catholic Church does believe that the scriptures are a word from God with authority. Their catechism states, "God is the author of Sacred Scripture. The divinely revealed realities, which are contained and presented in the text of Sacred Scripture, have been written down under the inspiration of the Holy Spirit."[1] "The inspired books teach the truth. … the books of scripture firmly, faithfully, and without error teach that truth which GOD, for the sake of our salvation, wished to see [confided] (sic) to the Sacred Scriptures."[2]

So, the individual Catholic person should be bound by conscience to accept what the Bible says to be authoritative and true for them.

Begin with what Jesus Christ taught about authority. Read Matthew 5:18. "For verily I say unto you, until heaven and earth pass, one jot or one tittle shall in no wise pass from the law, till all be fulfilled" (KJV). What does this verse say about the issue of authority? Note that a "jot" is the smallest letter in the Hebrew alphabet, and a "tittle" is the smallest stroke that distinguishes one letter from another. This would be like changing a capitol *O* to a capitol *Q* in the English language.

Continue with Luke 24:44. "Now He said to them, 'These are My words which I spoke while I was still with you, that all things which are written about Me in the Law of Moses and the Prophets and the Psalms must be fulfilled.'" What does this declaration by Jesus Christ add to the issue of biblical authority?

Read John 5:45–47; 12:44–50, and discuss what they add to the issue of the Bible as authority?

Also, what the apostles declare about the topic is extremely important. There are several helpful passages. Here ae some passages that might be helpful in certain situations. Acts 2:24–36; Acts 13:16–41; 2 Peter 1:20–21; 2 Peter 3:1–2; 2 Peter 3:15–16; 2 Timothy 3:14–17.

After you have a good understanding of what these verses are saying, you are ready to use them in your evangelism. If the person is willing, keep going through the different passages as far as seems necessary until he or she seems to understand and accept the Bible as authority for what the person believes regarding his or her own salvation. For some this might be a short journey, and for others a longer period may be required.

Issue: What is one's authority for discovering and determining what salvation truth is? For most Roman Catholics, it is whatever the Roman Catholic Church (their priest) says.

For many, perhaps most, Roman Catholics, crucial to them understanding and accepting the saving gospel is their acceptance of the Bible as final authority. They begin to understand that they have been taught something different by their church. It is here that they must transfer their confidence from the church to the Bible as final authority. If they are having trouble making this transition, lead them to Mark 7:1–13, a powerful passage on tradition versus the Bible as authority. When they decide the Bible is right and the church is wrong, a *key* milestone in their spiritual understanding has been reached. Hints that transition is occurring would be indicated by comments like, "You know, the Catholic Church teaches that Mary had no children other than Jesus, but that isn't what the Bible says." Or "I didn't quite believe that the pope is infallible." Or _____.

Having experienced this spiritual transition in the lives of numbers of people, several examples of responses are sealed in my memory. One person was surprised that Jesus Christ and the New Testament authors had so much to say about the authority and importance of the Bible. As she became engaged in serious Bible study, one lady indicated that it seemed there was one Jesus she had understood through her church involvement and another Jesus revealed in the Bible. This fact was surprising to her and presented an internal spiritual challenge until she chose to accept that the Bible revealed the real Jesus.

Also, some were surprised to learn Jesus Christ had sufficiently paid for our sin; therefore, no other payment needed to be made or could be added to what Jesus had done. I remember one man saying that he suddenly realized the sin-paying work of Jesus was enough. Others were surprised by what can be called the "illuminating power of the Holy Spirit" in bringing them new and important understanding from the pages of holy scripture. One such example was the light on the face and joy in the heart when they understood a passage like Ephesian 2:8–9. "For by grace you have been saved through faith; and that not of yourselves, it is the gift of God; not as a result of works, so that no one may boast."

Having been thoroughly indoctrinated into a system that advocated the need to merit eternal life, it was amazingly liberating to learn that grace is *unmerited,* and that saving faith doesn't include any kind or number of self-works. I remember one person saying that she had kept on trying to climb the ladder to salvation but would always climb two rungs and fall back three.

These and many stories like them could be shared, illustrating the importance of understanding and accepting the holy scriptures as final authority in important spiritual matters like the way of salvation.

FOCUS WELL ON THE SUFFICIENCY OF THE CROSS WORK OF CHRIST

Official Roman Catholic doctrine declares the necessity of the death of Christ as payment for sin. For most Roman Catholic people, the *sufficiency* of the work of Christ on the cross is a missing ingredient. Perhaps it's another indication that church doctrine and practice have replaced salvation truth as a way to heaven in the minds of most Roman Catholics.

This is a major deficiency in their thinking. We need to be diligent here as a witness.

When I speak of sufficiency, I mean that the physical and spiritual death of Jesus Christ on the cross was and is the only adequate payment for the penalty for sin that God pronounced on mankind. It satisfied the just demands of God. Therefore, He can now justify, forgive us of our spiritual rebellion as well as all the individual sins we have committed, and deliver us from condemnation while remaining a just God and provide spiritually dead people eternal life (Romans 3:26). When Christ cried, "It is finished!" as recorded in John 19:30, He declared His substitutionary death to be the final and sufficient sacrifice for sin. One may choose to trust in this sufficient sacrifice for deliverance from condemnation, for forgiveness, or for eternal life—or one may reject this provision and spend eternity separated from God in hell and never complete the payment.

It appears that many, if not most, typical Roman Catholic people believe in the necessity of the cross of Christ for salvation but don't believe in its sufficiency. According to the normal Roman Catholic layperson's understanding of salvation truth, a penalty had to be paid for sin, and the gate toward heaven had to be opened, but ongoing payment for sin is required—penance in time and/or purgatory after death.

Thus, when evangelizing these lost souls, it's important to focus on the sufficiency of the cross work of Christ to have paid the final, once-for-all sufficient penalty for our sin as our substitute.

Illustration: Recently at a friend's funeral service, this author interacted with a man who responded to the saving-grace gospel in a Bible study I led almost forty years ago. He referred to one statement I made one evening, a statement that kept going through his mind as he drove home and even for the next days. He remembers it being like this: The death of Jesus Christ for our sins was necessary *and enough!* This truth was the key truth that enabled him to understand the gospel and respond to Jesus Christ as Savior. His testimony was quite encouraging. Sometimes we forget just how important such core truths are to those who don't yet understand.

The topic of sufficiency is important enough to include the following summary of material on this subject in the book of Hebrews.

BRIEF SUMMARY OF TEACHING IN HEBREWS REGARDING THE SUFFICIENCY OF CHRIST

We find in Hebrews 9–10 excellent biblical support for the view of sufficiency, which declares the one death of Christ as satisfactory payment for sin for all time. A prominent theme of Hebrews is the superiority of Christ. In His person He is superior to the prophets, the angels, and Moses. In His role as a priest, He is superior in qualification (5:1–10) and in His work He is superior to any Old Testament sacrifices or law-keeping for a God-appeasing righteousness purpose (9–10).

The important term *hapax* occurs in 9:26–28. "The basic meaning of *hapax* in the New Testament is acquired when it refers to uniqueness of Christ's work as something which cannot be repeated."[3] In Hebrew

9:27–28, the author declares, "And inasmuch as it is appointed for men to die once and after this comes judgment, so Christ also, having been offered once [*hapax*] to bear the sins of many, will appear a second time for salvation without reference to sin, to those who eagerly await Him."

As certain as it is that men die once, it is likewise certain that Christ was to be offered only once as a sacrifice for sin, for our sin(s). Do you understand what this biblical text is saying?

The Hebrews 10:10–12 verses provide additional powerful insight. "By this will we have been sanctified through the offering of the body of Jesus Christ once for all. And every priest stands daily ministering and offering time after time the same sacrifices, which can never take away sins; but He, having offered one sacrifice for sins for all time, SAT DOWN AT THE RIGHT HAND OF GOD."

Substitutionary sacrifices offered by the Old Testament priests were only temporary; thus, day after day and year after year, they continued the practice, never permanently solving the sin problem. But Jesus Christ as priest and sacrifice did it once and then "sat down," because the necessary sacrificial work was accomplished—totally and finally.[4]

Several respected commentators understand these passages in this manner. Regarding Hebrews 9:24–26, Hodges states, "The heavenly ministry of Christ called for a thoroughly sufficient, one-time sacrifice. This is precisely why He appeared once for all [hapax]."[5] Regarding Hebrews 9:27–28, Hodges further states,

> With this observation (of vss. 24–25), eschatological realities come into focus. Humans are sinful creatures destined to die once, and after that to face judgment. But this danger is turned aside by the fact that Christ

was sacrificed once (*hapax,* cf. v. 26) to take away
the sins of many people. The recurrence of "once"
(9:26, 28) and of "once for all" (7:27; 9:12; 10:10)
stresses the finality and the singleness of Christ's
sacrificial work in contrast with the repeated Levite
ministrations. In addition, the "once"—sacrifice of
Christ (vv. 26, 28) compares with the "once"—death
of each person (vs 27).[6]

This would be the common conservative evangelical view of these
portions in Hebrews. And this is clearly what the biblical text is
saying.

Additionally, a remembrance of these famous words by Jesus
Christ on the Cross adds additional support to this idea. There He
proclaimed, "*It is finished!*" (John 19:30). This is the translation of
the one Greek word *tetelestai.* Papyri receipts for taxes have been
recovered with this single word written across them meaning "paid
in full." Jesus Christ had paid the full price for our redemption.

Therefore, the "once for all" death of Christ was sufficient to pay for
the sins of mankind for all time. Efforts at rejecting the sufficiency of
His one death and even attempting to add meritorious works to earn
salvation have been described by unmistakably disapproving terms.
Note Hebrews 10:29. An effort to do so is behaving like one who has
"trampled under the foot the Son of God." This phrase "trampled
underfoot" "denotes contempt of the most flagrant kind."[7] Further
there are religious people that consider this death of Christ as "unclean"
or unholy" (Hebrews 10:29), meaning that the cross experience of
Christ was "no better than the most common death." [8] Or to say it
another way His death had no more specific worth than the blood of
any ordinary person.

It is incredible to me that anyone within Christendom would affirm that the once for all death of Christ is not sufficient to have paid the penalty for all of our sins.

It is incredible to me that anyone within Christendom would seek to add to this one death of Christ any kind of religious practice, any work(s), anything in order to merit eternal life.

God the Father is saying, "I have offered my Son!" How can anyone say: "It is not enough."

If you are in a group discuss with them the above material on the sufficiency of the cross work of Christ. Is it as important at this author thinks it is? Why or why not?

Note below the testimony of Joey Fasullo, recorded in New Orleans in 2004.

> Hello, my name is Joey Fasullo. I was brought up as a Catholic and the Catholic Church baptized me as an infant. I made my first communion and made my confirmation while in Middle School. I went through the Catholic schools including through Catholic High School and Graduated from a Catholic College. My family went to church on Easter and Christmas as they were not necessarily religious. But they brought us up with strong moral values and beliefs, but they did not go to church every Sunday.

Shortly after getting married my wife and I decided that we needed to practice the "faith" we were going to have and raise children. So, we returned to the Parish Church where we were both brought up and married. As we exited the church that day I turned and said to my wife, "Can't Get No Satisfaction." That's exactly the way I felt as I went through the motions. I knew the drill. I just didn't feel like it was getting anything out of the service. As a child I remember going to confession to purge myself of my sins. I would exit the confessional with a fervent heart and felt myself free from sin and in good favor with God. It's human nature to fall, stumble and sin again and just hope I wouldn't die before I went to the priest for confession again.

A friend of ours invited us to a Bible study that was led by Pastor Miller. We attended week after week, and I was amazed. Pastor Miller answered every one of our questions with a verse directly from the Bible, sometimes two or three verses. As a young person the nuns would tell us to take it on faith whenever we asked the tough questions. I just wanted to validate and to be sure that what I was believing was the truth. After all, my time in eternity is a long time. My wife and I attended the Bible study for quite a long time. We would stay after and visit with our friend that hosts the study. John would bring out his Bible and point out truths from the Bible emphasizing what Jesus said.

It took me awhile to get it. Much of what I heard was the same information I already knew. I knew Jesus died on the cross for my sins and that on the third day He rose again from the dead. I could recite the Apostles Creed and all the foundational truths of Christianity. I vividly remember hearing the words "Jesus died once for all for you." Then we read John 3:16, *For God so loved the world that He Sent His only begotten son that whosoever believes in him shall not die but shall have eternal life.* It was then that I finally realized that Christ died for me. He bore my sin upon Himself on the cross in the sacrifice that was both sufficient and enough to make me holy and acceptable in the eyes of God. It was like opening up my mind and it finally all made perfect sense. Nothing I could do myself could earn saving favor with God and gain me Heaven. That I was a sinner and would be so until the day I die; that I would never on my own power be good enough to make it into heaven. God knew this and that mankind could never be good enough to enter His holy presence. God had a perfect plan to restore my fellowship with him solving my sin problem. He sent His perfect Son who had no sin to die in my place to pay the penalty for my sin once and for all. It was my friend John that finally led me to salvation.

[Note added by Larry Miller: Some thirty-five years following this time in Joey's life, I returned to New Orleans to conduct the memorial service for Joey's friend John. At that service Joey reminded me that the most significant and helpful thing he remembered hearing me say during those several weeks of Bible Study were the words "Christ's death was both sufficient and *enough*."]

It was when I personalized what Jesus did on the cross for me that I finally realized how much He loved me and that if I was the only sinner in the world, He would have suffered the agony of calvary's cross just for me. That's a loving God so I decided to give my heart to Jesus and trust Jesus and the sacrifice He made on the cross for my eternal salvation. I prayed that night and confessed to God that I knew I was a sinner and make me a child of God. I knew I wasn't worthy, but I accepted his free gift of Salvation at that moment. It was like a weight of the world was lifted from me. I felt truly clean for the first time in my life. It was fantastic. It was like a joy I had never known

From that day forward I slowly but surely developed a more intimate personal relationship with God. I know now that the Holy Spirit lives in me. I know now that when he looks at me he does not see the sinner but sees his perfect Son Jesus Christ. Life continues to have its ups and downs but now I know that God is in control of every detail of my life. He brings me through trials and He is perfecting me experientially, teaching me to become more like his Son Jesus. I know now that God has a purpose and plan for my life. I have a desire to please him and submit to his will. I have a good God and I know that God loves me and that He will never forsake me. I know that He only wants what is best for me. How grateful I am to have found saving grace of God and know I am a child of God and have the assurance of spending eternity with my heavenly Father.

Discuss this testimony.

What is included in this testimony that emphasizes the importance of the principle of cultivating the soil of the lost Roman Catholic person's heart through relationship development, highlighted in chapter six?

Did you note the importance of the sufficiency of the cross work of Jesus Christ?

What else caught your attention as you read the testimony?

How did this testimony make you feel?

MINI DECISIONS DURING THE SEED-SOWING PHASE

There appear to be several decision points each person will or may progress through as you cultivate the soil of the person's heart, preparing to start the seed-sowing process. It appears to likewise be true as you go through the seed-sowing phase leading to the "harvest" time. Below is a list of possible such decisions? What do you think about the list? What would you add to the list or remove from it? Why?

1. The person has a positive attitude toward the Bible.
2. The person chooses to investigate the Bible.
3. The person chooses to believe the Bible and accept it as final authority.
4. The person has decided the Roman Catholic Church is wrong in some dogmas.
5. The person decides the Roman Catholic Church isn't the only way to heaven.
6. The person understands and accepts the biblical definition of the gospel, particularly the sufficiency of Christ.
7. The person understands the concepts of works and grace from a biblical perspective.
8. The person has a positive attitude toward the gospel. At this point he or she will often respond in saving faith, which moves the person into the "harvesting" category.

Make a list of five people you know whom you believe to be lost. Try to identify where you think they are along the way in this decision process.

Names	Where Are They in the Decision Process?
_____	_____
_____	_____
_____	_____
_____	_____
_____	_____

Chapter 8

HELP THE PERSON RESPOND TO JESUS CHRIST IN A SAVING WAY

We need to be able to present the gospel clearly to anyone of any background.

Don't forget the principle of one planting, one watering, and God providing the increase (fruit). First Corinthians 3:6–7 states, "I planted, Apollos watered, but God was causing the growth. So then neither the one who plants nor the one who waters is anything, but God who causes the growth." One normally doesn't plant and harvest on the same day.

It *is* an amazingly joyful experience when someone is born from the kingdom of darkness into the kingdom of light, from death to life, and from hell to heaven as destiny (Luke 15:1–10). Those involved in evangelism (and remember, it is our goal to get every possible believer involved) will want to be an agent to help the individual exercise saving trust in Jesus Christ as soon as possible or practical.

In a recent news item by David Goodman, president of Entrust, he referred to ministry in an area between the countries of Moldova and Ukraine. He quoted someone from there who said that in these days people come to Christ *one by one*. This material is included with the conviction that more time spent in cultivating the soil of a person's heart and doing well at sowing the gospel seed at the appropriate time will yield good results. The basic assumption is that many people will come to Christ one at a time. However, this isn't to rule out mass evangelism, or other methods of evangelism, methodologies that may remain effective in some cultures with certain people. Even then it's often true that hearts have been prepared through some kind of soil cultivation as described above. Billy Graham once stated that most people who walked forward in his crusades had been prayed for or had experienced relationships with believers before the harvest at the crusade. When people place saving trust in Jesus Christ as Savior anywhere at any time through any legitimate methodology, we all should rejoice. Again, this material emphasizes more the one-on-one or one-at-a-time response.

Based on some of the preceding material, it might appear that the process is too slow or that harvesting is downplayed. This isn't my intent. *I am convinced that increased attention to the matters discussed will increase the effectiveness of evangelism over the long term, including a better harvest.*

A PERSONAL STORY OF EXPERIENCE IN NEW ORLEANS

Here is an encouraging word about our church experience in New Orleans. After several years of ministry there our church consisted of about two-thirds former Roman Catholics, most of them reached with the grace-saving gospel by and through people involved in our church. During numbers of years, we baptized twenty to forty adults, most of whom were from a Roman Catholic background. Some might say, "Well, that isn't such a large number to be so pleased about." But for me and us as a church, it was a thrilling experience, obviously enabled by God Himself. Many times Aunt

Mary Ann, our very first nursery worker, said to me, "Oh, Pastor Miller, thank you for coming to New Orleans." I baptized her when she was in her sixties. Over the thirty years in New Orleans as pastor of that one church, we saw scores of people delivered from darkness to light, from condemnation to forgiveness, and from hell to heaven. Thanks be unto God. The approach I am outlining in this project does work if we are dependently obedient and "work it."

Though I indeed did work hard, the glory goes to God Himself, and much credit is given to the many faithful and effective co-laborers Jesus Christ brought together in that church.

What key applied truths and methodologies contributed to this joyful experience? A few are summarized here.

- From the front platform during Sunday morning worship, we regularly did things to emphasize the importance of evangelism. We never once gave a "walking the aisle" invitation. This isn't to criticize those who do so. We often included Sunday A.M. service testimonies by people telling their stories about becoming saved believers in Jesus Christ—some newer believers and by others who had been believers for decades. We were often offering evangelism training opportunities and upcoming harvest vehicles.

- We practiced what some have called "side-door evangelism" (that is, the people go out to do evangelistic ministry themselves) rather than front-door evangelism (inviting people to church so the professional can evangelize them). There isn't necessarily anything wrong with the latter. On the very first Sunday we met as a worshipping congregation, one young lady in her twenties trusted Christ as Savior.

- We provided periodic new opportunities for evangelism training. This included something like the methods and material provided by Larry Moyer and his Evantell ministry,[1] and "Evangelism Explosion," as developed by Pastor D. James Kennedy.[2] We didn't just do classroom kind of training but had coaches who walked with the trainees as they developed and gained more confidence in applying what they were learning.

- Along the way we began to understand the importance of caring and respectful relationships with lost Roman Catholic people. Sometimes these were family members. At other times they were work associates; sometimes they were other neighbors, school connections, and so forth. The people in their world.

- We also began to understand the importance of non-church location harvest opportunities of some kind. These included people inviting people in their world into their homes for a fixed number of weeks. Sometimes these might be called "Bible studies," but most often they were known as a "Discovery Series." Invitees came for, say, four weeks and asked any question they wished about religion, spirituality, or the Bible. I began with one group in a particular subdivision, intending to do the series for four weeks, but it continued for two years. The host or hostess couple, former Roman Catholics, were great people gatherers. Several of these invited guests trusted Jesus Christ as Savior during this period.

- We also did periodic larger harvest kinds of activities. This might include a non-church location friendship dinner at a restaurant or country club. People brought their unsaved friends as guests. We had a well-prepared testimony by one of our people and brought in an outstanding speaker. Sometimes this speaker preached evangelistically in our church on Sunday morning.

BIG POINT

This appeared to work, yielding regular converts. People were developing relationships on a regular basis, helping their friends make progress along the path of their mini decisions, and lovingly introducing Jesus Christ, the Savior, to them though life and gospel proclamation. Yes, to some this process may seem a bit slow, but it was productive, bearing much fruit. Remember, preparing the soil, planting the seed, then harvesting take place. Time is required.

· ·

It is my conviction that sometimes the witness can press forward on this issue before the person is ready to do so. The result can be an emotional response but not a real conversion, or the person may even be given a false sense of security.

However, the person needs to hear the gospel clearly and be encouraged to respond. Paul repeatedly exercised himself with strong efforts to persuade people (Acts 13:43; 17:2–3; 18:4; 19:8; 28:23) and exhorted us to do likewise (2 Corinthians 5:20). Caution: do not be inappropriately timid at this point. Sometimes people are ready to respond sooner in the process than we might think.

Discuss the scripture portions in the preceding paragraph. Thoughts?

The following material is intended to facilitate a transition into the gospel presentation as well as how to present the biblical grace gospel message clearly.

Here are suggestions for some good questions to use to lead them toward a gospel interaction. Do so prayerfully, and you will probably discern where they are regarding readiness to respond positively.

1. "Have you developed far enough in your spiritual life or journey to know that you would go to heaven when you die?" This question isn't accusing. It assumes something positive about the person's spiritual interest.

2. If the person says no, you could respond with something like, "Would you like me to show you in the Bible how you can know for sure you will go to heaven when you die?" If the answer is yes to this second question, then proceed to explain the gospel and invite the person to respond.

3. If the answer is yes to question one above, do not assume the person adequately understands. Ask him or her something like this: "When you face God, suppose He would ask you, _____ [name], 'Why should I let you into My heaven?' What would your answer be?" The person's answer to this question will tell you a great deal about what he or she understands. A lot of people will give an unacceptable answer at this point. You could respond with something like, "I can tell you have thought about this. But you may

not be totally clear on this point (or something like this, whatever is appropriate). May I use the Bible and show you?"

What else have you found to be effective as a way to introduce or make a transition to the gospel?

I cannot emphasize to you enough the importance of having a way to present the gospel clearly. Below is one of the well-known and, in my opinion, clearest ways a number of evangelicals go about presenting the gospel. And keep in mind the issue of grace, faith, and works, particularly for the Roman Catholic person.

GOSPEL PRESENTATION

Keep in mind that the person with whom you are communicating, if outside the family of God, has two most serious and desperate needs.

- He or she needs forgiveness for the penalty of sins.
- He or she is spiritually dead and needs new life.

Suggestion for a Sound Gospel Presentation

Larry Moyer developed this method,[3] called "Bad News Good News." A brief outline is included here. There are a "few" slight modifications.

> Question: Has anyone ever taken a Bible and shown you how you can *know for sure* you're forgiven of your sins and have eternal life? May I?

Statement: The Bible contains both *bad news* and *good news*.

The *bad news* is something about you.

The *good news* is something about God.

Let's look at the bad news first.

As you go through this process encourage them to use their own Bibles if they have one and are willing. But please be sensitive as you attempt to do so. Refer to this same reminder in chapter seven.

Now back to the bad news.

Bad News One

We are all sinners.

Romans 3:23, "For all have sinned and fall short of the glory of God."

"Sinned" means we have missed the mark. When we live, hate, lust, or gossip (or _____), we have missed the standard God set for us.

Suppose you and I were each to throw a rock and try to hit the north pole.

You might throw farther than I can, but neither of us would hit it. When the Bible says, "All have sinned and fall short," it means we have all come short of God's standard of perfection, and it is certain we will continue to fall short. In thought, words, and deeds, we haven't been perfect.

But the bad news gets worse.

Bad News Two

The penalty for sin is death.

Romans 6:23 says, "For the wages of sin is death."

Suppose you worked for me, and I paid you fifty dollars. Those fifty dollars were your wages. They are what you earned.

This biblical text concisely identifies the penalty for sin, namely death.

God condemns sinners to death. All people in their natural condition are spiritually dead—that is, separated from God because of their sin (Ephesians 2:1).

The Bible teaches that those who die in the spiritually dead condition will be sent into the second death, which is eternal separation from God (Revelation 20:11–15).

But …

There was no way you could come to God on your own. But God foresaw that men would sin, and even before creation, He planned to provide a way of salvation (1 Peter 1:18–21).

Good News One

God has provided for your eternal salvation.

A. Christ died for you.

Romans 5:8 says, "But God demonstrates His own love toward us, in that while we were still sinners, Christ died for us."

B. Christ lives to give eternal life.

Christ proclaimed that He is the source of eternal life (John 11:25; 14:6).

Suppose you are in a hospital, dying of cancer. I come to you and say, "Let's take the cancer cells from *your* body and put them into *my* body."

If that were possible, what would happen to me?

What would happen to you?

I would die, and you would live.

I would die in your place.

The Bible says Christ took the penalty we deserved for sin, placed it on Himself, and *died in our place.* Three days later, Christ came back to life to prove that sin and death had been conquered and that His claims to be God were true. Also, the resurrected Christ is our life—that is, our source of eternal life—and He is perfectly capable of giving us such life.

Just as the bad news got worse, the good news gets better.

Good News Two

You can be saved through faith in Christ.

Ephesians 2:8–9 says, "For by grace [undeserved favor] you have been saved through faith, and that not of yourselves, it is the gift of God, not of works, lest anyone should boast."

"Saved" in this context includes forgiveness and eternal life.

Very importantly, *faith* means "trust."

Q. What must you trust Christ for?

You must depend on Him alone to forgive you and give you eternal life.

Just as you trust a chair to hold up you through no effort of your own, so you must trust Jesus Christ to get you to heaven through no effort of your own.

But you may say, "I'm religious," "I go to church," "I'm a good person," "I help the poor," or "I don't do anything that's really bad."

These are all good, but good living—going to church, helping the poor, or doing any other good thing you might do—cannot get you to heaven. You must trust in Jesus Christ alone, and God will give you eternal life as a gift.

Note: For a Roman Catholic person, the issue of "faith" or "trust alone" without meritorious works as a condition for salvation is a huge point. An additional helpful verse to share is Titus 3:5, "He saved us, not on the basis of deeds which we have done in righteousness, but according to His mercy, by the washing of regeneration and renewing by the Holy Spirit."

Is there anything keeping you from trusting Christ right now? Is so, what might it be?

1. _____

2. _____

3. _____

Think carefully. There is nothing more important than your need to trust Christ.

Would you like to tell God you are *trusting in Jesus Christ as your Savior?* If you would, why not pray right now and tell God you are trusting His Son?

Remember! It isn't a prayer that saves you. It is trusting Jesus Christ that saves you. It isn't trusting in Jesus Christ plus some work that saves you. It is trusting Jesus Christ alone that saves you.

Dear God, I know I'm a sinner. I know my sin deserves to be punished. I believe Christ died for me and rose from the grave. I trust Jesus Christ alone as my Savior. Thank You for forgiveness and everlasting life I now have. In Jesus's name, amen.

What Just Happened?

John 5:24 explains, "He who hears My word and believes in Him who sent Me has everlasting life, and shall not come into judgment, but has passed from death into life."

Did you "hear" what God's word has to say?

Did you "believe" what God said and trust Christ as your Savior?

Does "has everlasting life" mean later or right now?

Does it say, "Shall not come into judgment" or "Might not come into judgment"?

Does it say, "Has passed from death" or "Shall pass from death"?

Eternal Life Is Based on Fact, Not Feeling

Memorize John 5:24 today.

What Do You Do Now?

Tell someone about your choice to place your saving trust in Jesus Christ.

Having trusted Christ as your only way to heaven, here's how to grow in your relationship with Him.

- Tell God what's on your mind through prayer (Philippians 4:6–7).

- Read the Bible daily to learn more about Him and learn from Him (2 Timothy 3:16–17). Start in the book of Philippians.
- Worship with God's people in a local church (Hebrews 10:24–25).
- Tell others about Jesus Christ (Matthew 4:19).

Some Other Gospel Presentations Evangelicals Use in the USA

- The Romans Road, which has been around for many years
- Evangelism Explosion, developed by Dr. James Kennedy of Fort Lauderdale, Florida
- The Bridge to Life developed by The Navigators

PRESERVING THE FRUIT

You probably know how to do this. But I cannot emphasize enough the importance of doing well. In our ministry in the USA, we didn't always do well enough here. The following suggestions represent a summary of our experience—what we did well and what we learned from not doing well.

- One-on-one follow-up is very important. The new convert will probably have lots of questions and doubts Satan placed in his or her mind. We don't leave a newborn baby alone to make it on his or her own. We should not do so with a new convert. Work hard at making certain he or she has understood the gospel. The person needs assurance that he or she is now in the family of God.

- Group involvement also becomes important. We would do four- to six-week sessions on assurances. We most often used some Navigator material (Navpress.com). You may have other similar material you prefer.

- Beyond basic assurances, we also provided Nav 2:7 courses (Navigator material) for developing discipleship. Again, we believe some sort of systematic basic discipleship study material is very important. You may have some other material you prefer. But choose the best you know to be available and go through it with newer believers. Also, sometimes "older" believers can benefit either by way of review, or perhaps they never had the opportunity or experience to study. Please do it.

- Encourage engagement with the Bible—read it, memorize it, study it.

- You know local church involvement is important. Help it happen. However, when reaching Roman Catholics, be a bit cautious about the person's need to immediately leave the Roman Catholic Church. I know this is a bit controversial, but I believe this needs to be a decision the person makes based on internalization of truth and the conviction or leading of the Holy Spirit.

- Encourage and instruct them regarding the importance of prayer.

Chapter 9

TELLING YOUR STORY

Adapted from Nav 2:7 Training Material by
The Navigators (navigators.org)[1]
Used by Permission

WHY PREPARE A PERSONAL TESTIMONY?

The apostle Peter challenged us, "Always be prepared to give an answer to everyone who asks you to give the reason for the hope that you have" (1 Peter 3:15).

One of the most effective tools you have for sharing your faith is the story of how Jesus Christ provided a way to have your sins forgiven and how He gave you eternal life and enriched your life. The apostle John wrote, "We proclaim to you what we have seen and heard." (1 John 1:3) John was testifying about his relationship with Jesus Christ.

When the apostle Paul stood before Agrippa (Acts 26), he spoke simply, logically, and clearly about his life before salvation, how he met Christ, and what his life was like after conversion. Paul's testimony takes three or four minutes to read aloud in a conversational manner.

In preparing your testimony, it's wise to write it out. However, the purpose shouldn't necessarily be to memorize it and give it verbatim. The purpose is to help you put into words some of the important and interesting details in your conversion. The choice of the right words, the flow of your story, and how to begin and end are all important.

As you begin this project, ask the Lord for wisdom and insight into just how to share your story. Your facilitator may offer some suggestions along the way.

Many people have chosen to prepare their testimonies in this manner, and they have considered it a beneficial part of their discipleship-development process. People have come to saving faith in Jesus Christ simply because people like you have sharpened their testimonies and have chosen to share with others. Often in the process of attempting to share Christ with someone, there may be some resistance or reluctance on the part of the other person to hear or receive the message. However, they often will be willing to listen to your story. It may seem less confrontive to them, and it is undeniably your story.

Trust God and work hard. Give time, thought, and prayer to this important part of your evangelism training.

PREPARING A PERSONAL TESTIMONY

Considerable time will be spent in this lesson to start the testimony preparation process. You will be challenged to continue working on it on your own after this session has been completed. You may also be asked to return for subsequent sessions to present your testimony before the class. (Note to facilitator: If the circumstance can work and you can do so, it would be helpful for you to meet with each person to hear and comment on his or her testimony before the person presents his or her testimony to the entire group.)

As you start this process, it will be your aim to complete and present your personal salvation testimony from an outline on a three-by-five card. The amount of time and effort it will take each person to prepare a personal testimony may vary greatly. This has little to do with intelligence or spirituality. It has everything to do with the complexity of your story. Some testimonies are extremely difficult to communicate clearly. Some must be condensed. Others need to be expanded. There are many factors that influence how long it will take you to complete your written personal testimony. We have found it very helpful to eventually be able to present a condensed version of your testimony in three to five minutes. This will force you to reduce to the most important elements. This may be prayerful hard work, but those who have done so are thrilled at the results. It will be rewarding to sense your own heart blessing as you present it. Also, it will be thrilling to have others blessed by hearing your story. Your attitude and how aggressively you do your work can make all the difference. Work hard! Pray for God's wisdom and guidance.

Now More on Effective Personal Testimony Preparation

Paul's testimony in Acts 26 is a biblical model you can follow in writing your own personal testimony. Paul's format in Acts 26 is as follows:

Lead-in	Verses 2–3
Before	Verses 4–11
How	Verses 12–20
After	Verses 21–23
Close	Verses 24–29

With your group, read each of these sections and discuss your observations about what you note as some of the more important points of Paul's presentation that should be helpful to you as you prepare your own testimony.

Helpful note. Combine information when you can.

  a. Poor: "Martha Smith, Nancy Van Buren, and her cousin Lane Matthews came by my office at Digital Binary Components Corporation."
  b. Good: "Martha and two other friends talked with me at work one day."
  c. Good: "After living in three states and attending four universities, I finally graduated and got an engineering job."

DEVELOPING THE BEFORE, HOW, AND AFTER SECTIONS

1. Before

    a. Many people's actions spring out of their unsatisfied deep inner needs. What were one or two of your unsatisfied deep inner needs before you came to know Jesus Christ? Some examples of inner needs are the following:

    —Lack of peace   —Desire to be in control   —Lack of significance
    —Fear of death   —Loneliness   —No real friends
    —Something missing   —Lack of security   —No motivation
    —No meaning to life   —Lack of purpose

    Were any of these true of you? What would you add to the list?

    Non-Christians are usually trying to satisfy their deep inner needs through unsatisfactory solutions. In the past, what unsatisfactory solutions did you use to try to meet those deep inner needs? As you develop your testimony, list positive as well as negative solutions you may have tried. Some examples are the following:

—Marriage/family	—Sports/fitness	—Hobbies/entertainment
—Work	—Money	—Sex
—Drugs/alcohol	—Education	—Wrong friends

Were any of these true for you? What else would you add?

b.   Also, along life's way we understand the concept of sin. Most have a God consciousness and an inner sense that some things are right, and some things are wrong. Read Romans 1:20–23 and record some thoughts regarding what this passage says about the topic of right and wrong or sinfulness.

Discuss with your group somewhere along the way of testimony preparation.

What sins were you aware of?

Remember, sin can be something you do that you ought not to do (sins of commission) as well something you ought to do that you are not doing (sins of omission). Anything else to add to your list?

2.   How?

a.   Describe the circumstances that caused you to consider Christ as the solution to your deep inner needs. Identify the events leading to your conversion. In some cases, this may have taken place over a period of time. What particular sin issue were you convicted of or became aware of, knowing you weren't pleasing God? What were those circumstances? How did you begin to think of Jesus Christ as a solution to this problem?

b. State specifically and clearly the steps you took to become a Christian. If there is a particular portion of scripture that applies here, it would be wise to include it. Remember it is the holy scriptures, the Bible, that is our source of authority and what gives us confidence and assurance.

c. Include the gospel clearly and briefly. Remember the key points to keep in mind.

    1. All have sinned.
    2. Christ paid sin's penalty.
    3. I was spiritually dead and needed a new life.
    4. Christ was raised from the dead and can give me new life.
    5. I cannot ever work for or earn this salvation I need.
    6. I chose to place saving faith in Jesus Christ.

3. After:

a. State how knowing Jesus Christ as your Savior has removed your feelings of guilt and given you hope for time and eternity.

b. State how you now know your past efforts to meet your inner needs were futile and that now Christ is meeting those needs. Share an illustration or two about the difference Christ has made in your life.

    c.   Point out that this doesn't mean all my problems have gone away. But I now have a new perspective and supernatural help in confronting them.

    d.   And now I am certain I have eternal life. Sometimes if you are giving your testimony to one person or a small group, they may at this point want to know more about this statement. Often, it's natural to move from your testimony into a clear presentation of the gospel.

    e.   Share something about your spiritual growth, development, and what activities or relationship contributed to such.

Having reviewed all the above material in your group with your facilitator, it's important that you go home and start working on your testimony right away. After you have thought through the above and jotted down some notes, write out your entire testimony. This is very important. Write it out and then read through it a few times. Keep working on it. Then read it aloud a couple of times.

Be prepared to meet with your group for the next session, at which time you will share your testimony with some other group participants.

GIVING YOUR TESTIMONY

With your group leader or facilitator and group members, arrange sufficient "other times" together to do well at accomplishing the following "testimony practices." Meet with your group and be prepared to read through your testimony either with your entire group or with two or three people in your group, depending on how your group leader chooses to do it.

In your meeting time and when you go home, start reducing your testimony to an outline on something like a three-by-five card. This will be difficult, but it will help you to keep the most important material in your shorter version of your testimony. It will greatly help to practice giving your testimony to your group member just by using the three-by-five card.

Pray for opportunities to share your testimony. You could do so to groups at church. You could do it when you're relating to unbelievers. Many people seem willing to listen to your story. Usually, it doesn't seem very confrontational and may give you more of a listening ear and responsive heart.

And even in today's postmodern world, it may be received with some level of respect because it is your story—a popular concept today.

Conclusion

THE JOY OF HARVEST

The right answer to the question, "How do I enter heaven and escape hell?" ought to be high on everyone's priority list. Because of the grace of God many of you know the right Bible-based answer to the question.

Also, most of my readers likely have friends and acquaintances who cannot give a confident answer to such an important question. And many of them may be Roman Catholics. Further, many of you have lacked a good understanding of what Roman Catholics are trusting for their eternal life. How do they think they will get to Heaven?

I know many of you have been hoping they could give a good and right answer. I understand why you would feel that way.

Review the following summaries included earlier in this book.

SUMMARY OF THE ROMAN CATHOLIC WAY OF SALVATION

Authority – They declare the scriptures to be the inspired Word of God.[1] However, in addition they believe authority is provided in/by:

> Apostolic Succession
> Tradition
> Hermeneutics (Interpretation of scripture)

Sacraments – They were established by Jesus Christ and there are seven of them, the most notable being baptism and the eucharist.[2] Partaking of the sacraments is required for salvation.[3] It is understood that as the priest pronounces the right words the recipient receives the grace benefits signified by the sacrament, such as forgiveness of sins and increased righteousness.

Justification – It is a process of infusion of righteousness as one participates in the sacraments. The Council of Trent document declares that justification is increased before God through good works.[4] The Council voted 32 to 5 to reject the view that righteousness is imputed. Therefore, a practicing Roman Catholic can never know when he or she has enough righteousness to enter heaven.

Grace – To this day for them grace is understood to mean merited favor. "Moved by the Holy Spirit . . . we can merit . . . the graces needed for . . . the attainment of eternal life."[5]

Faith – In the Roman Catholic documents they repeatedly make the point that grace and faith are not to exclude the concept of merit. They even declare that a person who thinks he can have salvation by non-meritorious faith alone is to be cursed. "Let him be anathema."[6]

SUMMARY OF BIBLE-BASED WAY OF SALVATION

Authority - The Bible, the Holy Scriptures, are understood to be the ultimate and final authority regarding salvation issues. It is considered to be a static, non-expandable foundation. There is no other authoritative revelation from God.

Sacraments - There are no sacraments in the sense that they are understood by the RCC. The term was not used by the apostles or Jesus Christ; it does not appear in our Bible. Jesus Christ did not establish the sacraments. Sacraments are not necessary for a person's salvation.

Justification - Justification means being declared innocent, not guilty. God can declare us so because the Cross work of Christ was fully sufficient to pay the full penalty for our sins. "It is finished" (John 19:30). We appropriate unto ourselves this justification by faith alone. At that point the righteousness of Christ is imputed, or credited, to our account.

Grace - Sourced in the immeasurable love of God salvation is provided to mankind as a free gift of superabounding grace. This is an unmerited grace not earned by keeping any set of moral laws or religious duty.

Faith - The necessity and benefits of salvation are appropriated or received by faith and faith alone. No self-works are required or even possible to earn this salvation.

With good loving care and a commitment to biblical accuracy, I have demonstrated that the Roman Catholic official way of salvation is contrary to that which is defined and defended by the Apostle Paul. Also, it is true that the way of salvation as declared by the Roman Catholic Church is that which dominates the thinking of most Roman Catholic people –it is what they hear from the Priests. Therefore, loving honestly requires me to conclude that most Roman Catholics do not understand the biblical grace saving gospel message. To enter heaven they desperately need to hear the gospel accurately and by faith alone respond to the offer of eternal life.

You have the opportunity to continue relating to your friends in a loving way. You can help them understand how to be certain of their eternal destiny. You could give them no greater gift than to pursue this opportunity.

I have labored at providing you the needed information about how to do this. It is my prayer than you will be enabled by God the Holy Spirit to use what is here provided and see numbers of your friends rejoice in their new-found saving understanding of the gospel. Remember the stories of Beth, Eileen, Cathy, and Joey.

And once again remember these words of the Apostle Paul. "For who is our hope or joy or crown of exultation? Is it not even you, in the presence of our Lord Jesus at His coming? For you are our glory and joy" (I Thessalonians 2:19,20).

Appendix A
THE ISSUE OF FEAR

Leighton Ford once wrote, "I'm an evangelist, and have been witnessing and sharing my faith since I was fourteen years old. I have preached to crowds of 60,000 people, and yet I still get nervous when talking to an individual about Christ." Yes, fear is common.

Larry Moyer, a noted evangelist in the United States,[1] has some helpful material for overcoming fear in evangelism. I include it here, with permission from Larry. It was very helpful to me when I was beginning this journey as a young Pastor.

OVERCOMING FEAR AND ACQUIRING INCREASED BOLDNESS

Question: How can I overcome my fear in sharing the gospel? Satan would like nothing better than to have believers live in fear of sharing Christ to the point that they never open their mouths to proclaim the life giving, greatest news in the world. The single biggest reason that believers don't evangelize is … "I'm afraid." Afraid of rejection, afraid of blowing the chance, afraid of questions, afraid of losing a friend, afraid of failing, or afraid of being labeled a religious nut! Fear in evangelism can make you wither like a plant without water, or it can choke you out like a plant surrounded by weeds.

Let's be clear on two points:

1) Greater is he that is in me that he that is in the world.
2) Fear in evangelism is (normal) !

Even the apostle Paul was not exempt from fear in evangelism, and he asked for boldness. What was it about Paul that helped him overcome fear and share the gospel with boldness, even in difficult circumstances? In I Thessalonians 2:1-10, Paul lays out four fundamental principles that we can apply to

help us overcome fear with boldness. He sets the scene for us in verse 2 by explaining that he and Silas were spitefully treated in Philippi. Note Acts 16:12-24. They were attacked, stripped, whipped, and bound in stocks in the public square. Certainly, they had reason NOT to be bold in the next town!

And yet, in Thessalonica, Paul says that "we were bold in our God to speak to you the gospel." Why were they bold? Read and study I Thessalonians 2:1-10. Discover in the verses as indicated below four principles for overcoming fear in evangelism. (I have included the answers for you.)

1. (vs. 2) The source of Paul's boldness was (God Himself) . It is all about Him and it all comes from Him.

2. (vs. 3) You know God's (message) .

What was it? (The gospel) -the word gospel means Good News.

Remember the angel at the birth of Christ in Luke 2 who said, "For behold, I bring you good tidings (news) of great joy which will be to all people." The message you have is:

- From God
- Good news
- For all people

What it was not

- From error – the ravings of a deluded fanatic
- Uncleanness – moral impurity
- Deceit – guile or trickery in order to capture a prey

Knowing that you have the right message of good news, that is, God's message, is a key principle in overcoming fear.

3. (vs. 4) You are God's _(messenger)_ .

- You are _ (approved)_ by God. You are approved. We are stewards of the gospel, given the opportunity to use His gospel to glorify Him.
- You are _ (entrusted)_ with the gospel. We are partners with Him and the job we have been entrusted with is the exciting one of telling someone else about Him.
- We are to be _ (pleasing)_ God. Our desire is to please the One who has approved us and entrusted us with His good news.

You are the one God wants to use—to partner with—to bring the good news of His Son to your lost friends. He wants you to have the joy of sharing in this task with Him. Satan is a master intimidator and will try any means to convince you that you are not worthy to share the gospel. God says you are. What a great gift. You are the one He wants.

4. (vss. 5-8) You have God's _(motive)_ .

   Paul shows the purity of his heart and motive—that of God's heart and motive. In these verses, he states three things that he was not motivated by and one thing he was motivated by in three ways.

   He was not motivated by:

   - _(flattering words)_ - speaking as an orator using empty compliments for selfish reasons—either to elevate himself or to convince them for his own gain.
   - _(cloak of covetousness)_ - covering up a greedy desire for converts to build his ego and/or money to fatten his wallet.
   - _(glory from men)_ - his own recognition.

   He was motivated by YOU. Four times in two verses he states his motivator—YOU—the non-believers of Thessalonica. He had this heart in three ways—he was:

   - _(gentle among you)_ - sensitive to them as a nursing mother cares for her children.
   - _(longing for you)_ - affectionate—he liked them and cared about their well-being.
   - _(caring)_ - they had become dear to him—he loved them.

Now, let's clear up some misconceptions.

Misconception 1

If evangelism scares you, then you don't love Jesus.

Response

Evangelism scares everyone. The issue is not are you afraid, but will you go ahead despite your fears.

I Corinthians 2:3; Ephesians 6:19-20

Misconception 2

You should not witness until your life is all it should be. You could do more harm than good.

Response

If you wait until your life is everything it should be, you will never evangelize. Satan knows that, so speak the message you have and live the life you should.

Misconception 3

He is disappointed with your results in evangelism, you have not led many people to Christ.

Response

It is not how many you bring to Christ that matters. That is God's responsibility. It is your faithfulness in bringing Christ to others that matters.

Note Acts 1:8; John 4:37.

Misconception 4 (Added by Larry Miller)

Obedient evangelism requires that we boldly preach the gospel to everyone as soon as we interact with him or her.

Response

We learn in previous material that this is often not the case. Often, we need to cultivate the soil and understand the person's mindset. We need to be sensitive to whether God, the Holy Spirit, has given us an open door of opportunity into the person's heart. Paul might have had this in mind in Colossian 4:3–4. And on some (perhaps many) occasions our overly aggressive and confrontive approach causes a resistance on the part of the non-Christian. However, an ambassador does have a message to speak for the one he or she represents, in this case Jesus Christ. Note 2 Corinthians 5:17–21.

Discuss: Have you struggled with any of these misconceptions?

Discuss: Which issue in the above material has helped you most in understanding how to overcome fear in evangelism?

Pray as a group for each individual to be able to make progress in this important area.

Appendix B
SUMMARY OF COLOSSIANS 4:2-6

The apostle Paul penned Colossians from prison in Rome. There he was a closely guarded prisoner of the Roman Empire, handcuffed to a Roman soldier twenty-four hours a day. His imprisonment had curtailed his opportunities to proclaim the gospel. But notice, even in prison he penned these exhortations to pray for opportunity to continue speaking the gospel to those around him.

So, the application to each of us is that, as spiritually alive people, as people of another kingdom, as people with indescribable spiritual wealth, as people with certainty of a good eternal destiny, we might be characterized as follows. And the application to what we are about in any evangelism training and activity is striking.

> A. Prayer (vv. 2–4)
> B. Conduct (v. 5)
> C. Speech (v. 6)

A. Prayer
"Devote yourselves to prayer, keeping alert in it with an attitude of thanksgiving; praying at the same time for us as well, that God will open up to us a door for the word, so that we may speak for the mystery of Christ, for which I have also been imprisoned; that I may make it clear in the way I ought to speak" (Colossians 4:2-4).

1. The Action of Prayer

   Pray for yourselves [implied] and for us—Paul, Timothy [1:1], Epaphras [4:12], and others—with devotedness or continually. "Devote" is a present-tense imperative with the idea of continuing steadfastly to give constant attention to (Acts 2:42), to be in constant readiness (Mark 3:9), to persevere, to be courageous.

2. The Attitude of Prayer

   "With alertness" means "to give strict attention, to be most watchful as we anticipate our Lord's Coming" (Matthew 24:42; Mark 13:35), as we ought to be in the face of our enemy Satan (1 Peter 5:8). The idea seems to be to take heed lest some calamity overtake you. Also, of course you must be awake, so be careful about "long prayers." Ha!

   With thanksgiving. Note Philippians 4:4–7.

3. Pray for Opportunity.

   God will do what He must do and what only He can do, which is to provide the right opportunities. "Open to us a door" means to furnish an opportunity to do something.[1] Note in Acts 14:27 that the implication is that a door of admission for the Word, an opportunity to speak the gospel, will be provided.

4. Pray for the Right Content.

   "The word" and "the mystery of Christ" seem to refer to the same content. Regarding the "mystery of Christ," note Ephesians 2:11–3:13, especially 3:6. It is that the Jews and

Gentiles are now to be "fellow heirs," "fellow members of the body of Christ," and "fellow partakers of the promise in Christ Jesus." Thus, in this age of grace, in this dispensation, something new—the universal church, the body of Christ, not new wine in old wineskins—is to be our experience. And it is for both Jew and Gentile. But note well that the agency or means is "through the gospel." Check 1 Corinthians 15:1–5.

Solutions to man's individual problem(s) and the problems of mankind throughout planet earth aren't just political, sociological, financial, and so forth but sin, for which *the gospel* is the answer.

Also, pray that, when we have opportunity to speak, we might speak to bring truth to light, to make it manifest, not to cloud it with a lack of clarity or to corrupt it with error.

Additional insight is provided by using the term "ought" in verse 4. It can mean something like we have an obligation to do something because it is a command or duty. Examples of such usage: Matthew 23:23; Luke 22:7; Acts 5:29; 1 Corinthians 8:2.

It can also mean something brought on by circumstances or by the conduct or attitude of others toward us. Examples: Matthew 26:35; Luke 19:5; John 4:4; Acts 27:21.

So, which meaning does it have in Colossians 4:4? That's perhaps difficult to conclude since in the context it could mean speaking due to an obligation to speak out as an ambassador of Christ or to speak with the words and sensitivities dictated by the person to whom you are speaking at this particular time in his or her life, or perhaps both meanings. I lean toward the latter view, which fits other exhortations and examples. We must speak what is appropriate for the occasion, what the person needs to hear at this time, based on the degree of openness the person has. Wuest translates, "As it is necessary in the nature of the case for me to speak."[2] In my experience this fits well. We need to discern "where the person is" in his or her understanding, receptivity, needs, and so forth.

It is somewhat like the idea contained in a word often used in our relationship with believers; that is *parakaleo*. This term means to be alongside and call out or speak. It implies that one is close enough geographically and/or relationally, so we know what is needed by the other person. The term is translated in the New Testament by such words as *comfort*, *exhort*, *encourage*, *admonish*—words that are different but appropriate for the occasion.

Applications:

1. In evangelism prayer is the first order for God to open the doors of opportunity, to open the hearts of those about whom you have concern. That is, ask God to do what only God can do. Be cautious about "going where God has not prepared the way."

2. We must be concerned about and be prepared to speak the right content.

    This certainly includes the necessity to be prepared to present the gospel clearly. See chapter eight for one example of a clear gospel presentation.

3. Also, and importantly as well, we need to be sensitive to the needs of the person to whom we are speaking, to what he or she is ready and most needs to hear at this occasion.

    Example: We could be declaring the gospel, and the person is thinking, "But that is just your opinion." Perhaps what the person needs now is a discussion on why we can trust the Bible as our authority. We could think of numbers of such examples.

    What are some you could think of?

B. Conduct or Wisdom Walk toward Unbelievers (v. 5)

"Conduct yourselves with wisdom toward outsiders, making the most of the opportunity."

"Conduct" is a present imperative, so it's more than a suggestion; it's something to be done regularly and consistently.

> "Conduct" is the idea of ordering one's behavior, and the context here is toward those who are lost, outside the body of Christ, the unbelievers.

> "With wisdom" seems to mean to conduct yourself in such a way that you don't give an unfavorable impression of the gospel.

> And be opportunistic. Wuest says, "To make wise and sacred use of every opportunity."[3] These would certainly include the opportunities God has provided.

Major Applications:

1. We do need to walk the walk alongside someone before we attempt to talk the talk.

    This could be called "incarnational evangelism." We are influencing others by how we live our lives. They watch.

2. We need to make the most of opportunities. And we're not here talking about always blasting people with the gospel. We need to be sensitive to numerous opportunities to favorably impress others with the value, truthfulness, and benefits of the gospel.

C. Speech (v. 6)

"Let your speech always be with grace, seasoned, as it were, with salt, so that you will know how you should respond to each person" (Col. 4:6).

Again, speech toward "outsiders" is in view.

It should be characterized by grace. This means speech that is gracious, pleasant, and sweet; the courtesy of conversation to favorably impress the unsaved.

And it should already (perfect tense) be prepared (a good reason for this manual and this study) so that speech will be seasoned with salt. The idea of seasoning is to prepare and arrange (perhaps the idea of preparation) but also to make savory, pleasant, wholesome. Salt was used to preserve food or to fertilize the land or both. So here is the idea of bringing forth fruit and good nourishment.

Perhaps this is similar to the idea in Ephesians 4:29. "Let no unwholesome word proceed from your mouth, but only such a word as is good for edification according to the need of the moment, so that it will give grace to those who hear."

And be prepared to personalize and individualize your speech for each person with whom God has provided opportunity.

Major Applications:

1. How we say something is often as important as what we say.

2. We need to study and know each person. Where is he or she? What are his or her questions? What issues do you need to be dealing with?

THE CHARGE TO EQUIP OR TRAIN

As I have indicated, often there are exhortations to do evangelism without the sufficient provision of training to effectively accomplish evangelism. Is this true? Yes or no?

How does this make you feel?

A key passage for this kind of training or reproduction ministry is 2 Timothy 2:2. Let's study 2 Timothy 2:1–2 together. Read through the entire epistle from Paul to Timothy, known as 2 Timothy. It is the last epistle Paul wrote before the Romans executed him in Rome. It must be very important. Now prayerfully read, reread, and read again 2 Timothy 2:1–2. Make several observations. Whom does the pronoun "you" refer to? What are the main action verbs in the passage?

When Paul says "entrust these" to what is he referring? Hint: check the previous context as well as the immediate passage.

What is to be the source of Timothy's strength?

What is the goal or measure of one the passage describes as "faithful"?

What is the intended result of having what Paul taught Timothy and others?

How many generations of believers do you find in the text? Identify them.

If you are studying this material with a group, discuss with your group members this question. What does this passage say about the topic of training others for evangelism?

Also consider in prayer before God, our Father, how you might apply this important text in your own ministry. Write down some thoughts.

Now let's do some study of a central text on the importance of equipping or training others, Ephesians 4:11–16. Read and reread Ephesians 4:11–16. Also include the first ten verses of Ephesians 4 in your reading to help you with the context and your overall impressions of this passage.

> 11. And He gave some as apostles, and some as prophets, and some as evangelists,and some as pastors and teachers, 12 for the equipping of the saints for the work of service [some translations read ministry], to the building up of the body of Christ: 12 until we all attain to the unity of the faith, and of the knowledge of the Son of God, to a mature man, to the measure of the stature which belongs to the fullness of Christ. 14 As a result, we are no longer to be children, tossed here and there by waves and carried about by every wind of doctrine, by the trickery of men, by craftiness in deceitful scheming; 15 but speaking the truth in love, we are to grow up in all aspects unto Him who is the head, even Christ, 16 from whom the whole body, being fitted and held together by what every joint supplies, according to the proper working of each individual part, causes the growth of the body for the building up of itself in love (Eph 4:11-16).

What might be some reasons why I included this as a central text on this very important topic?

In verse 11, to whom does "He" refer?

There is some debate regarding the terms "pastors and teachers" in verse 11. Some people understand this to be two different people, gifts, or offices. Others consider these two terms to describe one gifted person or office. Harold Hoehner wrote what has been recognized as "the most detailed and comprehensive treatment of Ephesians ever written."[1] He wrote, "Because one article is used for both of these gifted people, scholars have debated over the centuries as to whether they represent two different gifted persons or one person with a combination of two gifts." Hoehner concludes that all pastors are to be teachers, though all teachers are not to be pastors. We will assume this understanding to be the correct one. Some have referred to this office or ministry role as "pastor-teacher."

Also, we understand that the gifted persons called "apostles" and "prophets" no longer exist. It is certainly true that the church was built on the foundation of the apostles and prophets (Ephesians 2:19–22). But there is no longer a need for these gifted persons because we have God's completed, written revelation, the holy scriptures. We understand that there is today a need for the evangelist and the pastor-teacher, as understood above.

Now, according to verse 12, what does the text say about a key purpose for which they are given to the "body of Christ" or "the church?"

Let's think about this. What have you normally thought the function of an evangelist or a pastor-teacher to be?

Have you understood that a major intended purpose of these gifted persons is to equip others to do ministry?

Yes or no? Why have you had this understanding?

By now you should understand that a major intended function of these gifted persons is to equip others for ministry or service. Do you agree?

Who are the "saints" of verse 12?

How do you know? Hint: note Ephesians 1:1.

Who is to be doing much of the work of service, which results in the "building up of the body of Christ"?

What does the phrase In Ephesians 4:16 "according to the proper working of each individual part" add to the discussion of all believers being equipped to engage in the "body-building" process?

What is your understanding of the concept of "building up"?

Here are a couple of suggestions for how to better understand the term. It is very important to our understanding of a healthy church and how it becomes one. We can check out some other passages where it is used, such as Ephesians 2:21; Romans 14:19; 15:2.

Also, if you have access to some sort of Bible dictionary or other source of word meanings, it can help you gain a better understanding. The term refers to the act of building something still in process and not yet complete. And here it is, the building up of a living and growing organism composed of living believers, the body of Christ, the church. As the term is defined in *Thayer's Dictionary of Greek Terms*, it refers to edifying or the act of one who promotes another's growth in Christian character and virtue. This would refer to a qualitative growth of each believer as well as the church as a whole. Some also see the possibility of the idea of quantitative growth or the adding of "living stones" (new believers) to the "spiritual house" (the church) as in 1 Peter 2:5. This view would be consistent with the "evangelists" in 4:16 being church equippers. What would an evangelist equip believers to do? It would be to "evangelize," the result of which would be new believers added to the church.

Consider that Ephesians 4:13–15 describes a "built-up" group of believers. Carefully read through these verses and list the different qualities that would characterize a "built-up" group of believers. It will be an impressive list.

Note some key application points.

- Christ has given gifted spiritual leaders to the church to do, among other things, a ministry of equipping others to serve or minister.
- And who is to do the ministering or serving in the church?
- Are you in the process of equipping others to serve or minister, or are you in the process of being equipped?
- What application does this principle have in the area of evangelism? Remember, we have concluded that Jesus Christ wants all believers to be engaged in evangelism.

Are we convinced this includes *everyone* ministering effectively in evangelism?

Do you agree? How does this make you feel?

If you are meeting with a group discuss it with them.

As you seek to apply this important principle, does it require any changes in your attitude, ministry philosophy, time allotment, and so forth? Take some personal quiet time and think about it. Ask God, the Holy Spirit, to minister to you according to your need and His great desire for your growth and success.

If meeting with a group pray together with them.

It is a joyful experience to become equipped and equip others to be engaged in evangelism obediently, lovingly, and effectively. What does Paul say in 1 Thessalonians 2:19–20 as support for this statement? "For who is our hope or joy or crown of exultation? Is it not even you, in the presence of our Lord Jesus Christ at His coming? For you are our glory and joy."

Endnotes

Introduction

1   Larry E Miller, *Roman Catholics: Saved or Lost?* (Bloomington, IN: WestBow Press, 2020). Hereafter referred to as "My Book."

Chapter 1 From Hope to Anguish

1   Richard N. Ostling, "The Second Founder of the Faith" (<u>Time</u>, September 29, 1986).

2   John Hannah, *Our Legacy,* (Colorado Springs, Colorado: NAVPRESS, 2001), 270.

3   Augustine, <u>Enchiridion</u>, chap. 8, par. 65. Translated and Edited by Albert C. Outler, 1955. <u>Enchiridion</u> was written near the end of Augustine's life thus a good source for his "settled" convictions and views.

4   H. J. Schroeder, *The Canons and Decrees of the Council of Trent*, (Rockford, Illinois: Tan books and Publishers, 1978), iii.

5   Normally the Roman Catholic "general councils" are considered to be those ecumenical (versus provincial councils where bishops of a church province or region meet) councils which are assemblies of patriarchs, cardinals, presiding bishops, abbots, male heads of religious orders, and other judicial persons, nominated by the pope. The purpose of such general councils is to define doctrine, reaffirm truths of the Faith, and eradicate heresy. Such general councils about which we are most likely familiar are Council of Trent (1545-1563), Vatican I (1869-1870) and Vatican II (1962-1965).

6   Walter M. Abbott and Joseph Gallagher, *The Documents of Vatican II* (New York: New York Guild, 1966), 703-04.

7   Ibid., 706.

8   David Wells, *Revolution in Rome* (Downers Grove, IL: InterVarsity Press, 1972), 5. However, it later appeared that this optimism had

been unjustified. According to official Roman Catholic thinking, the statements of a Council like Vatican II are to be authoritative and to be followed Further, according to the strictest hierarchal Roman Catholic view the statements of such a Council cannot ever be changed. As an example, there was no change included regarding their official view regarding justification. See chapter 3 in this book..

9   An outstanding discussion of evangelical identity is presented in *The Spectrum of Evangelicalism*, ed. Collin Hansen and Andrew David Naselli (Grand Rapids: Zondervan, 2011).

10   Document published in 1995 with title *Evangelicals & Catholics Toward a Common Mission Together* (Dallas: Word Publishing, 1995). Hereafter it will be identified as "Evangelicals and Catholics Together" or by ECT. See My Book, pages 44-51, for amplification of and controversy surrounding its content.

11   ECT, xx111.

12   According to *Vine's Expository Dictionary of New Testament Words*, 1940, the term *kosmos,* translated "world" in 2 Corinthians 5:19, can have several different nuances of meaning. He lists seven of them. The two of the seven mentioned by different interpreters as possibilities for 2 Corinthians 5:19 are first "the present condition of human affairs, in alienation from and opposition to God," and second, "Gentiles as distinguished from Jews, such as used in Romans 11:12, 15, or used where the meaning is that all who will be reconciled." (Here Vine uses 2 Corinthians 5:19 as an example.) So yes, the term *world* in 2 Corinthians 5:19 could potentially refer to human, civil society that needs to be reconciled. However, it more likely means that the individuals within society who need salvation can be reconciled. Vine understood this to be the meaning in 2 Corinthians 5:19. The Arndt and Gingrich *Greek-English Lexicon* does likewise. Furthermore, applying the principle of contextual interpretation to a quick reading of 2 Corinthians 5:14–21 leaves little doubt that "individuals" are meant. Those who use 2 Corinthians 5:19 as supportive of their version of social action or societal reordering have a long interpretive hill to climb to demonstrate that this is the intended meaning.

13   D. A. Carson, *Christ & Culture Revisited* (Grand Rapids, Michigan: Eerdmans, 2008).

14   Wayne Grudem, *Politics According to the Bible* (Grand Rapids, Michigan: Zondervan, 2010).

15 Edwin A. Blum, "John," in *The Bible Knowledge Commentary* (Wheaton, Illinois: Victor Books, Scripture Press Publication, 1983), 333.

16 David Wells, *The Courage to be Protestant* (Grand Rapids, Michigan: Eerdmans, 2008), 1-7.

17 Ibid., 7–8.

18 Hannah, *Our Legacy,* 18.

19 Walter M. Abbott and Joseph Gallagher, *The Documents of Vatican II* (New York: New York Guild, 1966), 703-04.

20 John Hardon, *The Catholic Catechism,* (Garden City, NY: Doubleday and Company, 1975). This book has the normal official notifications declaring that it is free of doctrinal error.

21 Hardon, 271.

22 Hardon, 254

23 Hardon, 273-74.

24 Hardon, 274 .

25 Hardon, 274

26 Hardon, 274

27 George Barna, 2011 Report on the "State of the Church in America." *barna@barna.org*.

Chapter 2 Another Gospel: Authority and Sacramentalism

1 Kenneth Kantzer, "American Catholics: What They Believe," *Christianity Today*, November 7, 1986, 26.

2 Ibid., 27.

3 Ibid.

4 *Catechism of the Catholic Church* (New York: Doubleday, 1995). All future references to "Catechism" will be this Doubleday, 1995, edition.

5 Abbott and Gallagher, *Documents of Vatican II*, 39–43.

6 *Catechism*, par. 869–870.

7 Historically this hasn't been the understanding of many others within the broader "Christian" Church. See the article by Robert D. Culver, "Apostles and the Apostolate in the New Testament," *Bibliotheca Sacra* 134:534 (April–June 1977): 131–43. Culver's thesis is that "the nature of the qualifications rendered the office untransferable. Thus the 'office' is restricted to the apostolic age." He summarizes six essential features of the apostolate, which make it impossible for anyone after the first century to be considered an apostle as advocated by those who promote apostolic

succession, since this is done by the official Roman Catholic Church dogma. Culver further stated that "none of the Scriptures cited" by Roman Catholic efforts really support their claim. He also directs those with further interest to the article "Succession, Apostolical," *Cyclopedia of Biblical, Theological, and Ecclesiastical Literature,* ed. John McClintock and James Strong, 12 vols., reprint ed. (Grand Rapids: Baker, 1970), 10:5–7.

8   Catechism, par. 105. Compare 80, 81, 107.

9   Hannah, *Our Legacy*, 24–27.

10 *Catechism*, par. 81.

11 Abbott and Gallagher, *Documents of Vatican II*, 117.

12 Ibid., 29.

13 Ibid. Also, cf. *Catechism*, par. 92.

14 Kenneth J. Collins and Jerry L. Walls, *Roman but Not Catholic* (Grand Rapids, Michigan: Baker Academic, 2017). 29. Also these authors state that they have drawn this "sacred canopy" term from Berger's celebrated book *The Sacred Canopy: Elements of a Sociological Theory of Religion*, reprinted ed. (New York: Anchor Books, 1990).

15 My Book. 122-127.

16 My good and reliable source is book by James G. McCarthy, *The Gospel according to Rome (*Eugene Oregon, Harvest House Publishers,1995). pages 184-198.

17 *Catechism,* par. 411.

18 *Ineffabilis Deus* by Pope Pius IX, 1854.

19 See McCarthy, page 196 for an explanation of this issue.

20 Abbott and Gallagher, *Documents of Vatican II*, 117–118.

21 *Catechism*, par. 113.

22 Ibid., par. 891

23 Ibid., par. 499.

24 *Catechism*, par. 1113.

25 *Catechism*, par. 1114.

26 *Catechism*, par. 1129.

27 Abbott and Gallagher, *Documents of Vatican II*, 146–49, 152. Also see t*he Catechism*, par. 1120, 1256.

28 *Catechism*, par. 1213, 1215, and other portions.

29 Ibid., par. 405 and other portions.

30 Ibid., 1084.

31 Catechsim, par. 1211.

32   Gustav Stahlin, *"hapax, ephapax"* in *Theological Dictionary of the New Testament,* ed. Gerhard Kittel (Grand Rapids: Eerdmans, 1966), 1:381.

33   Zane Hodges, "Hebrews" in *The Bible Knowledge Commentary: New Testament,* ed. John F. Walvoord and Roy B. Zuck (Wheaton, IL: Victor Books, 1983), 804.

34   Ibid., 803.

35   Ibid. "eschatological" means a study of the end times. "Levite ministrations" means the perpetually offered Old Testament sacrifices.

36   F. F. Bruce, *The Epistle to the Hebrews,* (Grand Rapids, Michigan: Eerdmans Publishing, 1964), 259.

37   McCarthy, 125-176.

38   Catechism, par. 1413.

39   McCarthy, page 153.

40   Ron Rhodes, *The 10 Most Important Things You Can Say to a* Catholic (Eugene, Oregon: Harvest House Publishers). pp. 85-86.

41   Mark A. Noll., and Carolyn Nystrom, I*s the Reformation Over?* (Grand Rapids: Baker Academic, 2005), 46–47.

42   Hannah, *Our Legacy,* 276.

Chapter 3 Another Gospel: Justification, Grace and Faith

1   Alister McGrath, *Justification by Faith* (Grand Rapids: Zondervan, 1988), p. 96.

2   H. J. Schroeder, *The Canons and Decrees of the Council of Trent,* (Rockford, Illinois: Tan books and Publishers, 1978).

3   Normally the "general councils" are considered to be those ecumenical (versus provincial councils where bishops of a church province or region meet) councils which are assemblies of patriarchs, cardinals, presiding bishops, abbots, male heads of religious orders, and other judicial persons, nominated by the pope. The purpose of such general councils is to define doctrine, reaffirm truths of the Faith, and eradicate heresy. Such general councils about which we are most likely familiar are Council of Trent, Vatican I (1869-1870) and Vatican II (1962-1965).

4   Schroeder, *Council of Trent,* iii.

5   5 Schroeder, *Council of Trent,* 42,45.

6   Klaas Runia, "Justification and Roman Catholicism," in *Right with God,* ed. D. A. Carson (Grand Rapids: Baker, 1992), 204–5.

7   *Catechism*, par. 2010. Other statements supporting this viewpoint can be provided.

8   Trent, 43, canon 12.

9   Trent, 43, canon 9.

10   *Catechism*, par. 1815.

11   *Catechism*, par. 1816

12   I surveyed 400 former Roman Catholics who were active in evangelical churches in South Louisiana. My primary goal was to determine what methodologies were most helpful toward them coming to saving faith in Jesus Christ. The research results have contributed to that which is included in the following chapters.

13   Catechism, par. 105. Compare 80, 81, 107.

14   *Catechism*, par. 1113.

15   Ibid, 1114

16   Schroeder, *Council of Trent*, 42,45.

17   *Catechism*, par. 2010. Other statements supporting this viewpoint can be provided

18   Trent, 43, canon 9.

Chapter 4 The Biblical Way of Salvation

1   William Hendriksen, *Exposition of Galatians,* New Testament Commentary (Grand Rapids, Michigan: Baker Book House, 1968), 37.

2   Hendriksen, *Exposition of Galatians*, 20. Also, Donald Campbell, "Galatians," in *The Bible Knowledge Commentary: New Testament*, ed. John F. Walvoord and Roy B. Zuck (Wheaton, IL: Victor Books, 1983), 588.

3   F. F. Bruce, *The Epistle to the Galatians: A Commentary on the Greek Text* (Grand Rapids, Michigan: Eerdmans, 1982), 31.

4   Ibid., 31–32. Also Hendriksen, *Exposition of Galatians*, 16–20.

5   I accept the common understanding that the genitive case for *Christ* (*Christou)* is an objective genitive; therefore, the text means the person's faith is to be in Christ.

6   Gorge V. Wigram, *The Englishman's Greek Concordance of the New Testament* (Grand Rapids: Zondervan), 157.

7   William F. Arndt and F. Wilbur Gingrich, *A Greek-English Lexicon of the New Testament* (Chicago: University of Chicago Press, 1957), 196.

8   Ibid.

9   Ibid., 751.

10 Ibid., 751.

11 The names "Christ Jesus" and "Christ" in this verse are commonly understood as objective genitives, meaning that the object of the person's faith is to be Christ Jesus. So they are translated "faith in Christ Jesus"" and "faith in Christ."

12 Gordon H. Clark, "Faith," in *Baker's Dictionary of Christian Ethics*, ed. Carl Henry (Grand Rapids: Baker, 1973), 234–35.

13 Joseph Henry Thayer, *Thayer's Greek-English Lexicon of the New Testament*, reprint of 1989 edition (Marshallton, DE: The National Foundation for Christian Education), 150.

14 Ronald Blue, "James," in Walvoord and Zuck, *The Bible Knowledge Commentary: New Testament*, (Wheaton, IL: Victor Books,1983), 825.

15 R. V. G. Tasker, *The General Epistle of James* (Grand Rapids: Eerdmans, 1956), 63.

16 Blue, "James," in Walvoord and Zuck, *The Bible Knowledge Commentary: New Testament*, 826.

17 Robert A. Pyne, "Justification by Faith" (unpublished notes from Theology 404, Dallas Theological Seminary, 1991), 92.

18 Pages 102-106.

19 Arndt and Gingrich, *A Greek-English Lexicon*, 196.

20 Pastor Steve Foster, Community Bible Church, Baton Rouge, Louisiana, October 24, 2021.

Chapter 5 What to Do Now? Prepare to Sow the Saving Gospel Seed

No endnotes in this chapter

Chapter 6 Prepare the Soil by Engaging the Lost Person

1   According to *Thayer's Lexicon*, portions where the root word for "light" (*phos*) appears it occurs with the meaning "the saving truth embodied in Christ and by his love and effort imparted to mankind."

2   The term translated "convince" in the NASB means "to convince of the truth."

3   Term *regeneration* means "rebirth, the production of a new life."

4   Tom Constable, "*Notes on 1 Corinthians*," Soniclight.com.

Chapter 7 Sow the Gospel Seed

1 Catechism, par. 105. Compare 80, 81, 107.

2 *Catechism, 107.*

3 Gustav Stahlin, "*hapax, ephapax*" in *Theological Dictionary of the New Testament*, ed. Gerhard Kittel (Grand Rapids: Eerdmans, 1966), 1:381.

4 Zane Hodges, "Hebrews" in *The Bible Knowledge Commentary: New Testament*, ed. John F. Walvoord and Roy B. Zuck (Wheaton, IL: Victor Books, 1983), 804.

5 Ibid., 803.

6 Ibid. Eschatological means a study of the end times; Levite ministrations are the perpetually offered Old Testament sacrifices.

7 F. F. Bruce, "The Epistle to the Hebrews," (Grand Rapids, Michigan: Eerdmans Publishing, 1964), 259.

8 Ibid.

Chapter 8 Help the Person Respond to Jesus Christ as Savior

1 Larry Moyer, *Seeds: from Sowing to Reaping,* (Dallas: Evantell).

2 Evangelistic training ministry begun in 1962 by D. James Kennedy, Ft. Lauderdale, FL. e*vangelismexplostion.org.*

3 Moyer, *Seeds: From Sowing to Reaping.*

Chapter 9 Telling Your Story

1 The Navigators, P.O. Box 6000, Colorado Springs, CO. 80934. Phone number: (719) 598–1212/navigators.org.

Conclusion The Joy of Harvest

1 Catechism, par. 105. Compare 80, 81, 107.

2 *Catechism*, par. 1113.

3 Ibid, 1114

4 Schroeder, *Council of Trent,* 42,45.

5 *Catechism*, par. 2010. Other statements supporting this viewpoint can be provided

6 Trent, 43, canon 9.

Appendix A The Issue of Fear

1   Larry Moyer, *Seeds: from Sowing to Reaping* (Dallas: Evantell).

Appendix B Summary of Colossians 4:2-6

1   Thayer, *Thayer's Greek-English Lexicon*, 48.
2   Kenneth Wuest, "Ephesians and Colossians," Wuest's Word Studies, vol. 1, (Grand Rapids: Michigan: Eerdmans, 1973), 234.
3   Ibid.

Appendix C: The Charge to Equip or Train

1   Clinton E. Arnold, Talbot School of Theology, in a comment about Harold W. Hoehner's book *Ephesians: An Exegetical Commentary* (Grand Rapids: Baker Academic, 2002).

Bibliography

Abbott, Walter M., and Joseph Gallagher. *The Documents of Vatican II.* New York: New York Guild, 1955.

Allen, Kenneth. "Justification by Faith." *Bibliotheca Sacra* 135 (April–June 1978).

Ankerberg, John, and John Weldon. *Protestants and Catholics: Do They Now Agree?* Eugene, OR: Harvest House, 1995.

Arndt, William F, and F. Wilbur Gingrich. *A Greek-English Lexicon of the New Testament.* Chicago: University of Chicago Press, 1957.

Arnold, Clinton E. Comment about *Ephesians: An Exegetical Commentary*, by Harold W. Hoehner. Grand Rapids: Baker Academic, 2002.

Augustine, *Enchiridion,* Translated and Edited by Albert C. Outler, 1955.

Barna, George. *2011 Report on the State of the Church in America. barna@ barna.org.*

Blue, Ronald. "James." In *The Bible Knowledge Commentary: New Testament*, edited by John F. Walvoord and Roy B. Zuck. Wheaton, IL: Victor Books, 1983.

Blum, Edwin A. "John." In *The Bible Knowledge Commentary: New Testament*, edited by John F. Walvoord and Roy B. Zuck. Wheaton, IL: Victor Books, 1983.

Bruce, F. F. *The Epistle to the Galatians: A Commentary on the Greek Text.* Grand Rapids: Eerdmans, 1982.

Campbell, Donald. "Galatians." In *The Bible Knowledge Commentary: New Testament*, edited by John F. Walvoord and Roy B. Zuck. Wheaton, IL: Victor Books, 1983.

Canons and Decrees of the Council of Trent. Translated by H. J. Schroeder. London: Herder, 1941.

Carson, D. A. *Christ & Culture Revisited.* Grand Rapids: Eerdmans, 2008.

Catechism of the Catholic Church. New York: Doubleday, 1995.

Clark, Gordon H. "Faith." In *Baker's Dictionary of Christian Ethics.* Grand Rapids: Baker, 1973.

Collins, Kenneth J., and Jerry L. Walls. *Roman but Not Catholic.* Grand Rapids: Baker Academic, 2017.

Colson, Charles, and Richard John Neuhaus, eds. *Evangelicals and Catholics toward a Mission Together.* Nashville: Word, 1995.

Constable, Tom. "Notes on 1 Corinthians." Soniclight.com.

Foster, Steve. "Summarizing Romans 1-5." Pastor Community Bible Church, Baton Rouge, Louisiana. pastor@cbcchurch.org.

"The Gospel of Jesus Christ: An Evangelical Celebration." Glendale Heights, IL: Committee on Evangelical Unity in the Gospel, 1999.

Grudem, Wayne. *Politics according to the Bible.* Grand Rapids: Zondervan, 2010.

Hannah, John. *Our Legacy: The History of Christian Doctrine.* Colorado Spring: NavPress.

Hardon, John. *The Catholic Catechism.* Garden City, NY: Doubleday and Company, 1975.

Hansen, Collin, and Andrew David Naselli, eds. *The Spectrum of Evangelicalism*. Grand Rapids: Zondervan, 2011.

Hendriksen, William. *Exposition of Galatians*. Grand Rapids: Baker, 1968.

Hodges, Zane. "Hebrews." In *The Bible Knowledge Commentary: New Testament*, edited by John F. Walvoord and Roy B. Zuck. Wheaton, IL: Victor Books, 1983.

Hoehner, Harold. *Ephesians: An Exegetical Commentary*. Grand Rapids: Baker Academic, 2002.

Kantzer, Kenneth. "American Catholics: What They Believe." *Christianity Today*, November 7, 1986.

Kennedy, D. James. Ft. Lauderdale, FL. *evangelismexplostion.org*.

Loe, Danny. "Developing Worldview-Wise Evangelists." Doctoral thesis, Talbot School of Theology, 2017.

McCarthy, James C. *The Gospel according to Rome*. Eugene, OR: Harvest House, 1995.

McClintock, John, and James Strong, eds. "Succession, Apostolical." In *Cyclopedia of Biblical, Theological, and Ecclesiastical Literature*. 12 vols. Reprinted edition. Grand Rapids: Baker, 1970.

McGrath, Alister. *Iustitia Dei: A History of the Christian Doctrine of Justification*. Vol. 1. Cambridge: Cambridge University Press, 1986.

McGrath, Alister. *Justification by Faith*. Grand Rapids: Zondervan, 1988.

Miller, Larry E. *"Methodologies Facilitating Roman Catholic Conversions."* Doctoral thesis, Dallas Theological Seminary, 1996.

Miller, Larry E. *Roman Catholics: Saved or Lost?* Bloomington, IN.: WestBow Press, 2020.

Moyer, Larry. *Seeds: from Sowing to Reaping*, Dallas: Evantell. lmoyer@
evantell.org.

Navigators, Colorado Springs, CO. navigators.org.

Noll, Mark A., and Carolyn Nystrom. *Is The Reformation Over?* Grand
Rapids: Baker Academic, 2005.

Ostling, Richard N. "The Second Founder of the Faith." *Time*, September
29, 1986.

Pyne, Robert A. "Justification by Faith." Unpublished notes from Theology
404, Dallas Theological Seminary, 1991.

Rhodes, Ron. *The 10 Most Important Things You Can Say to a Catholic.*
Eugene, OR: Harvest House, 2002.

Ryrie, Charles C. "A Synopsis of Bible Doctrine." *Ryrie Study Bible*, expanded
ed. Chicago: Moody Press, 1995.

Runia, Klaas. "Justification and Roman Catholicism." In *Right with God*,
edited by D. A. Carson. Grand Rapids: Baker, 1992.

.Stahlin, Gustav. "*hapax, ephapax.*" In *Theological Dictionary of the New
Testament*, edited by Gerhard Kittel. Grand Rapids: Eerdmans, 1966.

Tasker, R. V. G. *The General Epistle of James*. Grand Rapids: Eerdmans, 1956.

Thayer, Joseph Henry. *Thayer's Greek-English Lexicon of the New Testament*.
Reprint of 1989 edition. Marshallton, DE: The National Foundation for
Christian Education.

Vine's Expository Dictionary of New Testament Words. Westwood, NJ: Barbour.

Wells, David F. *Revolution in Rome*. Downers Grove, IL: InterVarsity Press,
1972.

Wells, David F. *No Place for Truth, Or Whatever Happened to Evangelical Theology?* Grand Rapids: Eerdmans, 1993.

Wells, David. *The Courage to Be Protestant.* Grand Rapids: Eerdmans, 2008.

Wigram, Gorge V. *The Englishman's Greek Concordance of the New Testament.* Grand Rapids: Zondervan.

Wuest, Kenneth S. *Wuest's Word Studies.* 3 vols. Grand Rapids: Eerdmans, 1973.

Printed in the United States
by Baker & Taylor Publisher Services